MAPS and SOCKS

A Walker's Miscellany

Tom Patterson

I am told that there are people who do not care for maps, and I find it hard to believe.

R. L. Stevenson

A walker only needs three socks - two on, and one in the wash.

(anon.)

Copyright © Tom Patterson 2013

This book is sold subject to the condition that it shall not, by way of trade or otherwise, be lent, resold, hired out, or otherwise circulated without the publisher's prior consent in any form of binding or cover other than that in which it is published and without a similar condition including this condition being imposed on the subsequent publisher.

The moral right of Tom Patterson has been asserted.

All rights reserved.

ISBN: 1484971175

ISBN-13: 987-1484971178

DEDICATION

To the memory of Arthur Hugh Sidgwick (1882-1917) whose *Walking Essays* (1912) were the starting-point of this Miscellany.

CONTENTS

	Foreword	1
1	What was the weather like?	5
2	Why did you go?	22
3	Where did you go?	39
4	What was it like in the hills?	72
5	How did you get there?	94
6	Did you have a rest?	123
7	What did you take with you?	137
8	Did you walk alone?	162
9	Or with companions?	170
10	What did you talk about?	177
11	And you sang?	183
12	Did you get tired of your companions?	190
13	Did you ever look back?	198
	Appendix (Arthur Hugh Sidgwick 1882-1917)	205
	Bibliography	209
	Index	215

FOREWORD

At least some printed work should mark
The walker and his wanderings,
The strides which lay the miles behind
And lap the contemplative mind
In calm, unfathomed ponderings.
From the Dedication, *Walking Essays* (Sidgwick 1912)

The author is but the accidental appendage of the tramp (Stephen 1901).

***

Over years of walking and back-packing, alone and in groups, on the flat and in the hills in various parts of the world, I collected books on walking, intending to turn my favourite excerpts into an anthology. I found that the book from which I had taken the greatest selection was *Walking Essays* (1912) by A. H. Sidgwick.* Although he is mentioned in other anthologies, I feel that he deserves wider recognition.

His style has not always been appreciated: 'too great a length and in a

---

* I have added a short biography (Appendix). With the permission of, and help from, his family I am preparing a full biography.

manner too jocular for modern taste' (Marples 1959). He certainly includes some digressions, but they come from his interest in different aspects of walking: physical fitness, games and sport, food and clothes. His love and knowledge of music show in various references, particularly to singing while walking. The 'comic irony' that runs throughout was characteristic of his time and of other members of his family - their contemporaries referred to it as 'sidgwickedness'.

He was a scholar, poet and essayist whose chosen career was in education, and through it all ran his love of walking and the happiness it brought him.

***

The first concern of walkers in all seasons is the weather. To them it is not just a topic of conversation but 'a matter of vital and compelling significance', whether they are soaking in a downpour or taking time out to rest in the sun or wrestling exultantly through a thunderstorm in the mountains.

Walkers rarely 'go for a walk', but rather set off to follow familiar tracks, or to see new sights in a spirit of independence and curiosity to know what is round the next corner, or for adventure (and perhaps to write about it). They seek old roads and follow the tracks of previous generations in the spirit of pilgrims, and the pub at Kirk Yetholm (at the end of the Pennine Way) becomes as important as the cathedral in Santiago. They go to escape from the tedious round of duty, or to work off depression, and they may find that walking encourages thinking and meditating. They feel the urge that takes them into the hills.

Walkers come to a friendly relationship with places where they walk; they can even enjoy walking in London. Further afield, they cross plains, walk along rivers, through forests, over downs and moors, through dales, round coasts, on long-distance paths, over passes, and up into the hills.

Hills/mountains have always had a powerful effect on those who look at them or move in them, varying from awe and terror to a strong attraction and a state of mind that might be described as mystical.

Walkers go by road, on old railway tracks, on long-distance paths, bee-lining across country (trespassing occasionally), running downhill, scrambling, taking short-cuts and getting lost. They may walk on into the night.

They may walk too fast and too far, but when they stop to rest they realise that 'if walking is rhythm, resting is melody'. (Starkie 1936) They may then find it hard to get going again.

Sleeping out may be an ecstatic experience, or it may rain.

Walkers vary in the equipment they take with them: some manage on what will fit into their pockets or a small satchel, others need a large pack hung with cooking utensils. Some prefer to go with a map in hand, others find it more exciting to do without. They may wear boots, shoes, or sandals, or may go barefoot, most wear socks, and some need a special hat or cap. A stick is useful in an emergency, and an umbrella is a sign of respectability. Food and drink become supremely important, and the weather is of no interest if the coffee-pot has been left behind.

Some prefer to walk alone and talk to themselves, or with one companion who can be trusted not to talk. Others enjoy walking in groups, and find that it encourages good talk.

Alone or in groups it is natural to sing - the soloist to celebrate the occasion, and the group in chorus to encourage flagging companions.

And if they tire of human company, they may prefer to walk with animals.

They can look back to see the changing scene at every stage of their walk, and when their walking days are over they can relive past expeditions in diaries and maps, in memory in times of stress or at peace alone or with old companions.

***

For the walker a map is often essential and it is customary to wear socks. But these, with boots and hard-boiled eggs, only belong to the mechanics of walking - important as a means to an end, but no more.

Many walkers experience something deeper, and Sidgwick describes this perfectly: his satisfaction in the physical and psychological effects of hard exercise, enhanced by his feelings for the countryside. At brief moments, and in various places (for him particularly in the hills of the Lake District), he feels something even more intensely. He describes this in a way that will be familiar to many walkers and mountaineers. Some of them have tried to write about it. They are all hard-put to explain it, although the physiologists may talk about serotonin and endorphins and the effects of hypoxia on the brain at high altitudes.

Their descriptions all tally: the feeling is always unexpected, occurring in any place and season, in any part of the world, sometimes on familiar walks, but more often in open country, in beautiful surroundings, and particularly in the hills. It is usually transitory - often only a flash - but always brings intense happiness, and a sense of well-being and that all's right with the world. Christopher Leach (1977) walking across country late in the day, turned and saw a line of poplars against a darkening skyline. *'And that old sense of something beyond the poplars, beyond even perhaps the skyline, came and for a second or so, glowed, and then was doused. It was, of course, as it always is - a glimpse of eternity. All time shrivels, you are at one with everything and with everyone that has ever lived.'*

And in John Buchan's experience:

'Moments, even hours, of intense exhilaration, when one seemed to be a happy part of a friendly universe... they came usually in the early morning or at sunset. I seemed to acquire a wonderful clearness of mind and to find harmony in discords and unity in diversity, but to find these things not as conclusions of thought, but in a sudden revelation, as in poetry or music. For a little, beauty peeped from the most unlikely wrappings and everything had a secret purpose of joy.

Scents, sights and sounds blended into a harmony so perfect that it transcended human expression, even human thought.

It was like a glimpse of the peace of eternity.'

(Buchan 1940)

***

This sense of something indefinable, stirred by my own experience at different times and in different places, has been of particular interest to me in the writings of walkers. It is a theme that runs through this anthology.

Tom Patterson

Oxford 2012

CHAPTER 1

WHAT WAS THE WEATHER LIKE?

The walker is, in virtue of his craft, above all things, sane and concrete, and therefore has little difficulty in observing the ordinary conversational traditions. But he is no blind acceptor of conventional limitations. On the contrary, he ever seeks to extend the limits of the conversational range, adding new topics of interest.

The first of these is the weather. For some obscure and probably discreditable reason, the weather is regarded as a trivial subject. In the more intense intellectual circles the weather is altogether taboo. If you mention it in Hampstead or Chelsea you are set down as a trifler and not asked again.

There is nothing really so interesting as the weather: nothing so omnipotent in its workings, so far-reaching in its effects, so inscrutable in its variety, so compelling in its fascination. And yet the heathen in his blindness - a fair description of the intellectual in his detachment - is pleased to rule out the weather as a triviality. He plumes himself on the universality of his social and political range, on his familiarity with the forces which lie behind the working of our ordinary life, but what force is so effectual and so omnipresent in every moment of every man's existence as the weather?

The intellectual plunges eagerly into the depths of art and literature and the drama, and talks with glib facility of the clash of cosmic forces; let him open a window and put out his head if he would know what a clash of cosmic forces really is. When kings are philosophers and philosophers are kings, their first act will be to reinstate the weather as a subject of supreme interest and importance, and the most sacred crown of unfading bay will be laid on the head of the meteorologist.

The struggle has already begun, and in the forefront of the fighting line are the walkers.

To them even more than other men the weather is a matter of vital and compelling significance.

There are already signs of the coming Restoration: even now, where two or three kindred souls are assembled, the weather begins to take precedence of other subjects. Recently, on a Saturday night, I happened to remark, in company, that as I walked to the house the wind was swinging round to the north, the sky was clear, the streets were dry, and there was promise of a brilliant Sunday. My host, who wished to discuss the merits of Zoroastrianism as a working creed for urban civilisations, became rather restive. But across the room I observed a man fixing an eager eye on me in total disregard of his neighbours. One look was enough. As soon as I had rebuffed the Zoroastrian with a few firmly enunciated prejudices, I moved across to my man and said, 'Do you know the track above Pickett's Hole?' He answered, 'Yes, but it's just been ploughed and wants marking out again.' So, as Touchstone says, we swore brothers.

(Sidgwick 1912)

The changing seasons

George Meredith once said to me that we should "love all changes of weather." That is a true word for walkers. Change in weather should be made as welcome as change in scenery. "Thrice blessed is our sunshine after rain." I love the stillness of dawn, and of noon, and of evening, but I love no less the "winds austere and pure." The fight against fiercer wind and snowstorm is among the higher joys of Walking, and produces in shortest time the state of ecstasy.

(Trevelyan 1913)

The north wind makes walking weather, and the earth is stretched out below us and before us to be conquered. Just a little, perhaps, of the warrior's joy at seeing an enemy's fair land from the hill-top is mingled with the joy in the unfolding landscape.

(Edward Thomas 1909)

No sort of weather, of course, can be dull anywhere - not even a great thaw - unless you have a dull mind to help it to bore you. But some sorts of weather are even more exciting than others. Most exciting of all, perhaps, in a city, are the first hours of romantic strangeness after a heavy fall of snow. While snow lies deep, the proportions of things are altered. Streets become much wider, especially if it be Sunday and not many people about. For the frontier between footpath and road is wiped out.

(Montague 1924)

The best time for walking is the winter. Many townsmen know little of the joys of winter walking, and only venture into the country in weather that is fine and warm. Winter, they think, is cold and wet. Cold it may be, and why not, pray? But wet it most certainly is not, at least, not especially wet. It rains far more in July and August than ever it does in December and January.

In the winter I can go across country. There is no undergrowth in the woods, there are no crops in the fields and no bracken on the slopes. One walks free and unencumbered and, broadly speaking, one walks where one likes.

And how much more one sees! In August the country is muffled under a blanket of dull green. The blanket spoils its shape and blurs its contours. The winds of winter have stripped the blanket away and laid bare the bones and naked structure of the countryside. And how lovely that structure is! I would give all the tender greens of young spring, all the gorgeous colours of the autumn woods' decay, for the bare boughs of an oak with its tracery of little twigs silhouetted against the dark red of an afternoon sky in December. The sun had just set and over against it, glimpsed through the infinitely lovely pattern work of the twigs, there is an evening star. There is a tang in the air, the earth rings hard under the feet, there will be a frost tonight. So home to a coal fire, with lamplight and curtains drawn, the kettle boiling on the hob, and crumpets for tea. What has summer to offer comparable to these winter delights?

(Joad 1946)

The walker in virtue of his craft is more intimately attuned to the temper of earth and sky, his soul and body are more of a piece, and his nature consequently responds with a subtler sympathy to the influences of weather. When a dry north-easter is stiffening the earth, the walker is a man of dour endurance, he attacks unpalatable tasks - arrears of letter-writing, the sorting of papers, the ordering of clothes - with readiness, almost with gusto. Then the wind dies down and the sky clears and a frost anti-cyclone sets in: forthwith he becomes a Stoic, thinking high and abstract thoughts, determining lofty resolutions, conceiving pure outlines of things. Then comes the herald of the most magical of all shifts, an Atlantic disturbance, there are hints of soft air from the south-west and smells of coming rain. At once the walker's nature responds: the iron resolutions begin to break down, the pure outlines are blurred, through every sense steals in the charm of detail and colour, he becomes less stoical, more humane, a fitter companion for the spring that is being ushered in without.

(Sidgwick 1912)

... a bright, sunny day, with some cloud and a cool wind. It was perfect weather for walking, and splashes of white in the hedges - not to mention an authentic minor third from a cuckoo - assured me that spring, though late, was come at last.

(Sidgwick 1918b)

After Christmas we are walking with the spring, with a new, young, whispering child-life in the old heart. Though the winds be cold and snow sweep over the land, we know that winter and death are spent. Spring comes, and then the tramp is marching with the summer. Summer is the year itself, all that the other seasons have laboured for. It is the glory of the year. Then may the tramp cease marching, for in the height of summer nature must also cease, must cease from going forward to turn back. He may rest in the sun and mature his fruits. Autumn is coming and all the year's beauties must yield to death.

Tramping all day through a sodden forest, I also experienced the autumnal feeling, the promise of rest, a new gentleness. All things which have lived through the summer welcome the autumn, the twilight of the long hot day, the grey curtain pulled down over a drama which is played out.

The tramp's summer is also over. He will not lie full length in the sun till the spring comes round again.

Many memories of past autumns came back to me. How many are the rich, melancholy afternoons of late October or early November, golden afternoons that occur year after year, when one feels one's thoughts parting from the mind easily and plentifully without urging, as over-ripe fruit falling at last since no one has grasped it before.

(Graham 1912)

Clouds

There was no breeze on the moor, but overhead white clouds were drifting quickly across the blue dome of heaven. I watched them come, stealing silently out of the west, squadron after squadron, witnessed their solemn procession above my head, saw them dissolve into the mist to the east. Big clouds and little clouds, there were, stately schooners in full rig, travelling in slow majesty, tiny yachts with wispy sails, speeding quickly to overtake the others, eager to make a race of it. I lay there, stretched out in the heather, and reviewed the fleet.

Clouds are the most transient of nature's creations. They come out of a clear sky, disintegrate before your eyes, vanish. You never see the same cloud twice. Every moment of its brief existence brings a change, a change of form or tint or texture, but its beauty remains constant to the end. The beauty of the clouds is there for us to see every day, if we are not too busy to look up, but if they peep at us over grimy buildings we shall not appreciate their grandeur so well. Seen from a mountain side, they have never the dull leaden effect which often characterises their appearance when they overhang the towns, they are never grey, never shapeless, never lustreless. Best of all is to look at clouds from above. Look down on them, not up at them, climb through them to Gable's summit on a wet day, and stand there in brilliant sunshine, looking across to Scafell or Pillar, rocky islands in a sea of billowing white. You will love clouds thereafter, be they ever so bleak and forbidding. For from above, they are always white, pure white. And always very beautiful.

(Wainwright 1986)

The Black Mountains were invisible, being wrapped in clouds, and I saw one very white brilliant dazzling cloud where the mountains ought to have been. This cloud grew more white and dazzling every moment, till a clearer burst of sunlight scattered the mists and revealed the truth. This brilliant white cloud that I had been looking and wondering at was the mountain in snow. The last cloud and mist rolled away over the mountain tops and the mountains stood up in the clear blue heaven, a long rampart of dazzling glittering snow so as no fuller on earth can white them. I stood rooted to the ground, struck with amazement and overwhelmed at the extraordinary splendour of this marvellous spectacle. I never saw anything to equal it I think, even among the high Alps. An intense glare of primrose light streamed from the west deepening into rose and crimson. There was not a flake of snow anywhere but on the mountains and they stood up, the great white range rising high into the blue sky, while all the rest of the world at their feet lay ruddy rosy brown. The sudden contrast was tremendous, electrifying. I could have cried with the excitement of the overwhelming spectacle. It seemed to me as if one might never see such a sight again. The great white range which had at first gleamed with an intense brilliant yellow light gradually deepened with the sky to the indescribable red tinge that snow-fields assume in sunset light, and then the grey cold tint crept up the great slopes quenching the rosy warmth which lingered still a few minutes on the summits. Soon all was cold and grey, and all that was left of the brilliant gleaming range was the dim ghostly phantom of the mountain rampart scarce distinguishable from the greying sky.

(Kilvert, 14 March 1871)

Mist

I enjoy a mist, it hides you so completely. If it is a mist on a mountain top, there is not a person in the world to witness your actions, you are alone as the first man on earth. A mist sharpens the faculties, as those of a blind man are sharpened. You sense danger, and there is nobody to help and advise, you have to use your wits and keep alert, for you are at a disadvantage with this baffling adversary. He has strange powers, this white monster. He can ensnare you so easily, he tempts you from the plainest of tracks, he makes the meekest of men adventurers. He can transform a blade of grass into a tree, a boulder into a huge crag, a sheep into a lion. Yes, it is good to walk in a mist now and again, and know your own limitations, and be scared by your own helplessness.

(Wainwright 1986)

In mist upon the mountains to keep the way, or to lose and find it, is one of the great primaeval games, though now we play it with map and compass.

When we see the mists sweeping up to play with us as we walk the mountain crests we should "rejoice" as it was the custom of Cromwell's soldiers to do when they saw the enemy. Listen while you can to the roar of waters from behind the great grey curtain, and look at the torrent at your feet tumbling the rocks down gully and glen, for there will be no such sights and sounds when the mists are withdrawn into their lairs, and the mountain, no longer a giant half seen through clefts of scudding cloud, stands there, from scree-foot to cairn, dwarfed and betrayed by the sun. So let us "love all changes of weather."

(Trevelyan 1913)

Rain

[the Lake District]

The country is, indeed, subject to much bad weather, and it has been ascertained that twice as much rain falls here as in many parts of the island, but the number of black drizzling days, that blot out the face of things, is by no means proportionally great. Nor is a continuance of thick, flagging, damp air so common as in the West of England and Ireland.

The rain here comes down heartily, and is frequently succeeded by clear, bright weather, where every brook is vocal, and every torrent sonorous.... Days of unsettled weather, with partial showers, are very frequent, but the showers, darkening, or brightening, as they fly from hill to hill, are not less grateful to the eye than finely interwoven passages of gay and sad music are touching to the ear.

Insensible must he be who would not congratulate himself upon the bold bursts of sunshine, the descending vapours, wandering lights and shadows, and the invigorated torrents and waterfalls, with which broken weather, in a mountainous region, is accompanied.

(Wordsworth 1835)

RAIN

WHEN the rain is coming down,

And all Court is still and bare,

And the leaves fall wrinkled, brown,

Through the kindly winter air,
And in tattered flannels I
'Sweat' beneath a tearful sky,
And the sky is dim and grey,
And the rain is coming down,
And I wander far away
From the little red-capped town:
There is something in the rain
That would bid me to remain:
There is something in the wind
That would whisper, "Leave behind
All this land of time and rules,
Land of bells and early schools.
Latin, Greek and College food
Do you precious little good.
Leave them: if you would be free
Follow, follow, after me!
When I reach 'Four Miler's' height,
And I look abroad again
On the skies of dirty white
And the drifting veil of rain,
And the bunch of scattered hedge
Dimly swaying on the edge,
And the endless stretch of downs
Clad in green and silver gowns,
There is something in their dress
Of bleak barren ugliness,

That would whisper, "You have read
Of a land of light and glory:
But believe not what is said.
'Tis a kingdom bleak and hoary,
Where the winds and tempests call
And the rain sweeps over all.
Heed not what the preachers say
Of a good land far away.
Here's a better land and kind
And it is not far to find."

Therefore, when we rise and sing
Of a distant land, so fine,
Where the bells for ever ring,
And the suns for ever shine:
Singing loud and singing grand,
Of a happy far-off land,
O! I smile to hear the song,
For I know that they are wrong,
That the happy land and gay
Is not very far away,
And that I can get there soon
Any rainy afternoon.

And when summer comes again,
And the downs are dimpling green,
And the air is free from rain,

And the clouds no longer seen:

Then I know that they have gone

To find a new camp further on,

Where there is no shining sun

To throw light on what is done,

Where the summer can't intrude

On the fort where winter stood:

Only blown and drenching grasses,

Only rain that never passes,

Moving mists and sweeping wind,

And I follow them behind!

(Sorley 1912)

[Charles Sorley, in his last year at school (1912), running on the Marlborough Downs. He was killed in 1915, aged 21]

I lay awake listening to the rain, and at first it was as pleasant to my ear and my mind as it had long been desired, but before I fell asleep it had become a majestic and finally a terrible thing, instead of a sweet sound and symbol. It was accusing and trying me and passing judgment. Long I lay still under the sentence, listening to words which seemed to be spoken by a ghostly double beside me. He was muttering: The all-night rain puts out summer like a torch. In the heavy, black rain falling straight from invisible, dark sky to invisible, dark earth the heat of summer is annihilated, the splendour is dead, the summer is gone. The midnight rain buries it away where it has buried all sound but its own. I am alone in the dark still night, and my ear listens to the rain piping in the gutters and roaring softly in the trees of the world. Even so will the rain fall darkly upon the grass over the grave when my ears can hear it no more.

(Edward Thomas 1913)

Like the touch of rain she was

On a man's flesh and hair and eyes

When the joy of walking thus
Has taken him by surprise:

With the love of the storm he burns,
He sings, he laughs, well I know how,
But forgets when he returns
As I shall not forget her 'Go now'.

Those two words shut a door
Between me and the blessed rain
That was never shut before
And will not open again.
(Edward Thomas 1922)

SORLEY'S WEATHER

When outside the icy rain
Comes leaping helter-skelter,
Shall I tie my restive brain
Snugly undershelter?

Shall I make a gentle song
Here in my firelit study,
When outside the winds blow strong
And the lanes are muddy?

With old wine and drowsy meats
Am I to fill my belly?

Shall I glutton here with Keats?
Shall I drink with Shelley?

Tobacco's pleasant, firelight's good,
Poetry makes them better.
Clay is wet and so is mud,
Winter rains are wetter.

Yet rest there, Shelley, on the sill,
For though the winds come frorely,
I'm away to the rain-blown hill
And the ghost of Sorley.

(Robert Graves 1918)

There is a long and instructive piece to be written by someone on how to walk for an hour or two in a downpour without at some stage being thoroughly depressed by it all, but not alas by me. In theory you can zip yourself up from head to toe in expensive semi-waterproof skins and face the bluster, striding out, turning over only amiable thoughts. This is how philosophical works are conceived but rarely if ever set to paper. The facts are always more prosaic.

(Hillaby 1976)

I set out again on my road, and was very much put out to find that showers still kept on falling. In the early morning, under such delightful trees, up in the mountains, the branches had given me a roof, the wild surroundings made me part of the out-of-doors, and the rain had seemed to marry itself to the pastures and the foaming beck. But here, on a road and in a town, all its tradition of discomfort came upon me. I was angry, therefore, with the weather and the road for some miles.

(Belloc 1902)

The walk in the rain, or worse than that, the walk through rain-laden thickets after the rain has ceased. the night slept in the rain when it begins to drizzle at eleven and you think nought of it, and to rain steadily at twelve and there is no refuge, and to pour gently at one and in torrents at two, and it is all the same because you are already as wet as can be - these are modifications of Nature's blessings, pleasant or unpleasant in themselves according to taste and breeding.

(Graham 1927)

The greatest enemy to the man who has to carry on his body all his wardrobe, is rain. As long as the sun shines he is indifferent, but if he is caught in a wet condition after sunset his is to be pitied. He does not fear any ill consequences to health from being wet through, as does his more fortunate brother, but he does not like the uncomfortable sensation of shivering and not being able to keep warm. This unsettled feeling is often made worse by an empty stomach. In fact a full stomach is his one safeguard against the cold, and he cares not then if the rain and the wind penetrate his clothes.

(Davies 1908)

Walking in rain is most enjoyable when you have made up your mind not to worry about keeping dry, and it is best to make this decision early. There is an invigorating quality about rain which makes you glow with exhilaration. Always turn your face to a weeping sky, not away from it, when you are in open country, and you have a tonic which will keep you in good humour for days.

(Wainwright 1986)

At all times I love rain, the early momentous thunderdrops, the perpendicular cataract shining, or at night the little showers, the spongy mists, the tempestuous mountain rain. I like to see it possessing the whole earth at evening, smothering civilization, taking away from me myself everything except the power to walk under the dark trees and to enjoy as humbly as the hissing grass, while some twinkling house-light or song sung by a lonely man gives a foil to the immense dark force. I like to see the rain making the streets, the railway station, a pure desert, whether bright with lamps or not. It foams off the roofs and trees and bubbles into the water-butts. It gives the grey rivers a demonic majesty. It scours the roads, sets the flints moving, and exposes the glossy chalk in the cracks through the woods. It does work that will last as long as the earth. It is about eternal business. In its noise and myriad aspect I feel the mortal beauty of immortal things. And then after many days the rain ceases at midnight with the wind, and in the silence of dawn and frost the last rose of the world is dropping her petals down to the glistering whiteness, and there they rest blood-red on the winter's desolate coast.

(Edward Thomas 1909)

Meredith has described once for all in *The Egoist* the delight of walking soaked through by rain (Trevelyan 1913):

'Rain was universal, a thick robe of it swept from hill to hill, thunder rumbled remote, and between the ruffled roars the downpour pressed on the land with a great noise of eager gobbling, much like that of the swine's trough fresh filled, as though a vast assembly of the hungered had seated themselves clamorously and fallen to on meats and drinks in a silence, save of the chaps. A rapid walker poetically and humorously minded gathers multitudes of images on his way. And rain, the heaviest you can meet, is a lively companion when the resolute pacer scorns discomfort of wet clothes and squealing boots. South-western rain-clouds, too, are never long sullen: they enfold and will have the earth in a good strong glut of the kissing overflow, then, as a hawk with feathers on his beak of the bird in his claw lifts head, they rise and take veiled feature in long climbing watery lines: at any moment they may break the veil and show soft upper cloud, show sun on it, show sky, green near the verge they spring from, of the green of grass in early dew, or, along a travelling sweep that rolls asunder overhead, heaven's laughter of purest blue among titanic white shoulders: it may mean fair smiling for awhile, or be the lightest interlude, but the water lines, and the drifting, the chasing, the upsoaring, all in a shadowy fingering of form, and the animation of the leaves of the trees pointing them on, the bending of the tree-tops, the snapping of branches, and the hurrahings of the stubborn hedge at wrestle with the flaws, yielding but a leaf at most, and that on a fling, make a glory of contest and wildness without aid of colour to inflame the man who is at home in them from old association on road, heath and mountain. Let him be drenched, his heart will sing. And thou, trim cockney, that jeerest, consider thyself, to whom it may occur to be out in such a scene, and with what steps of a nervous dancing-master it would be thine to play the hunted rat of the elements, for the preservation of the one imagined dry spot about thee, somewhere on thy luckless person!

The taking of rain and sun alike befits men of our climate, and he who would have the secret of a strengthening intoxication must court the clouds of the South-west with a lover's blood.'

(Meredith 1879)

Meredith is perhaps the Supreme Pontiff of modern country walkers: no soft lover of drowsy golden weather, but master of the stiffer breed who salute frost and lashing rain and roaring south west wind, who leap to grapple with the dissolving riddles of destiny. February and March are his months.

(Morley 1918)

Storm

It has been, let us say, a day that should be spring, and in the dark, wet copses there were thousands of primroses. All day the wind, and often rain and wind together, roared in the trees. The pale flowers were soaked and frayed and speckled with dust from the trees, and they hung down or were broken from their soft stalks. But the high land and the neighbouring sky exalt us. Even the sight of these tender blubbering petals ruined in the drenched grass was pleasant. We should have liked better to see them unspoiled and wide in the sun, but we did not wish them to be so, and their distress did but add to the glory of the storm and to our defiance, just as did the cowering of birds, of bowed trees, of whole woods, under the wild shadowy swoop of the mist and rain, and the valleys below us humbled, their broad fields, their upthrust churches and clustered villages overwhelmed and blotted out, and everything annihilated save the wind, the rain, the streaming road, and the vigorous limbs and glowing brain and what they created. We and the storm were one and we were triumphant.

(Edward Thomas 1913)

[in the Pyrenees]

A storm broke, and that with such violence that we thought it would have shattered the bare hills, for an infernal thunder crashed from one precipice to another, and there flashed, now close to us, now vividly but far off, in the thickness of the cloud, great useless and blinding glares of lightning, and hailstones of great size fell about us also, leaping from the bare rocks like marbles. And when the rain fell it was just as though it had been from a hose, forced at one by a pressure instead of falling, and we two on that height were the sole objects of so much fury, until at last my companion cried out from the rock beneath which he was cowering, "This is intolerable!" And I answered him, from the rock which barely covered me, "It is not to be borne!" So in the midst of the storm we groped our way down into the valley beneath, and got below the cloud.

(Belloc 1906)

It sometimes happens that a storm beginning in the afternoon will last all night ... it is an occasion when the art of idleness can be put aside. If it is necessary to walk a steady twenty miles to some place of shelter for the night, it is as well to set the mind to it.

After the first mile in the rain the tramp becomes pleasant, after five or ten miles, one begins to sing. One generally finishes in the highest of spirits, even though soaked to the skin.

(Graham 1927)

I had not gone far before the rain came down in torrents. There was no escape from it, no hope of shelter. The lane ever appeared before me out of a murky gloom, a wet, unending strip of dull grey between sodden banks. The deluge continued, lashing myself and all else into helpless resentment. We bowed before its impact, trees, shrubbery, self. Every drop that fell had its dart of venom, the hands and face were stung with icy barbs, for there was sleet in the air. The surface of the road was transformed into a living thing, so pitiless was the onslaught and so convulsive the recoil.

[out on to open moorland] No longer now could I escape the wind, if the demoniacal fury which greeted me could be called a wind. I saw sheets of rain flung across the dreary moor with hurricane force, I heard now the voice of the storm, no longer resisted but unrestrained and triumphant. There was moaning from afar, howling as the squally gusts hurled through the tormented sky, the wild shrieking rose to tumultuous crescendo as the gale tore overhead, and fell to a sobbing wail in the far distance. The din of the tempest was deafening, to me it was a roar of mockery. There was a giant madman loose on the moor, and his laughter was horrible...

I could never be certain when the next assault would come, nor from which direction. I could only be sure that each buffeting would bring a deluge of soaking rain, which would pour over me like a breaking wave, and that there would be a deafening bellow in my ear.

The moment I decided I was as wet as I could possibly be, I began to enjoy myself.

(Wainwright 1986)

CHAPTER 2

WHY DID YOU GO?

Walking is one of the many things whose history is not to be found in the historians. Being above all things human and intimate, it is naturally neglected. History has been mainly a catalogue of abstractions, interesting and even thrilling, but (to the walker) mostly irrelevant. The moment we begin to ask about the ordinary man of each period, what he was doing, and what he was thinking, and whether he liked walking, we are answered only in abstract terms.

(Sidgwick 1912)

Walking, like talking (which rhymes with it, I am glad to say), being so natural a thing to man, so varied and so unthought about, is necessarily not only among his chief occupations but among his most entertaining subjects of commonplace and exercise.

Thus to walk without an object is an intense burden, as it is to talk without an object. To walk because it is good for you warps the soul, just as it warps the soul for a man to talk for hire or because he thinks it his duty. But walk for glory or for adventure, or to see new sights, or to pay a bill or to escape the same, and you will very soon find how consonant walking is with your whole being. The chief proof of this is the way in which a man walking becomes the cousin or the brother of everything round.

There is no time or weather, in England at least, in which a man walking does not feel this cousinship with everything round. You may walk by night or by day, in summer or in winter, in fair weather or in foul, in rain or in a gale, and in every case you are doing something native to yourself and going the best way you could go. All men have felt this.

(Belloc 1911)

It is a gentle art, know how to tramp and you know how to live ... tramping brings one to reality. So when you put on your old clothes and take to the road, you make at least a right gesture. You get into your right place in the world in the right way.

(Graham 1927)

It is fairly clear that in all ages men have walked, more or less: indeed, this could be proved *a priori* from the anatomical structure of the leg. But it is equally clear that up to very recent times [1912] they have done so without the least knowledge of the value and purpose of walking. They have walked in a utilitarian spirit, to get somewhere, they have walked in a medical spirit, to improve their digestions, they have very rarely walked for the sake of walking, to realise themselves in a fine activity.

(Sidgwick 1912)

But even a man walking for exercise may forget his object and unexpectedly profit; he may surprise happiness by the wayside or beyond the third stile, and no man can do more.

(Edward Thomas 1913)

As I came down from the hill into the valley across the golden meadows and along the flower-scented hedges a great wave of emotion and happiness stirred and rose up within me. I know not why I was so happy, nor what I was expecting, but I was in a delirium of joy, it was one of the supreme few moments of existence, a deep delicious draught from the strong sweet cup of life. It came unsought, unbidden, at the meadow stile, it was one of the flowers of happiness scattered for us and found unexpectedly by the wayside of life. It came silently, suddenly, and it went as it came, but it left a long lingering glow behind as it faded slowly like a gorgeous sunset, and I shall ever remember the place and the time in which such great happiness fell upon me.

(Kilvert 1875)

John Cowper Powys has opened many eyes to the fact that in open country everywhere the delicate adjustment of foreground and background is the most subtle, the most perfect imaginable, for the foreground changes every second, whilst the background, the great horizon, changes so slowly that one can scarcely see the change. This succession of simple things, so obvious when you become conscious of them and yet so often neglected if you walk without concentration, is perhaps one of the most cogent arguments for walking alone.

In one of his gentle essays he says in effect that this is what we most desire in life, a ritual of human alternation in the foreground whilst behind it all, in the background, are the great processions, the things of which we are but a small part.

(Hillaby 1976)

True walkers have generally an air of being intent upon the business in hand: they do not talk much: and as a mere matter of fact they generally walk at a good round pace. But their pace is only accidental and subordinate to their main purpose. The full swing of the legs, like all physical activities, is a fine thing in itself, but it is merely physical. The great fact is that such an activity leads more directly than others to that sense of intimacy with air and sun and hills and green things, which is the walker's ideal. This sense of intimacy is not to be won by strolling, a man must do his best with his body before the gates are opened to him.

(Sidgwick 1912)

I wander about on foot for the sheer love of it, and there is no way of getting the feel of country other than by walking ... touch, physical contact, is the first sensation we're conscious of from the moment of birth onwards, and, if we're wise, we constantly renew that experience.

(Hillaby 1976)

This is the first day of the vacation and I am free to wander away from the tedious daily round of duty. Yesterday I did not feel as I do today, for I was still dominated by my conventional self. For months I had gone through life mechanically, paying meticulous attention to what my neighbours said of me. I enjoyed the monotonous rhythm of the daily task, for it prevented me from letting my thoughts dash recklessly away, like hey-go-mad.

Nobody who possesses a vagabond second self should ever put on his Gypsy clothes before the sun has set on the last day of term: they should be locked in the lumber-room with seven keys, otherwise they might behave like the magic shoes in the fairy tale and lead you a dance over the hills and far away.

(Starkie 1934)

What made it so worthwhile? After talking until two in the morning I thought I had got pretty close to the heart of the matter. Independence, I said. Walking means no pre-ordained schedules, no hanging about waiting for transport, for other people to depart. Alone with a pack on your back you can set off at any time, anywhere, and change your plans on the way if you want to.

(Hillaby 1972)

The principal motive of the wander-spirit is curiosity - the desire to know what is beyond the next turning of the road. In a sub-conscious way the born wanderer is always expecting to come on something very wonderful - beyond the horizon's rim.

(Graham 1927)

I have been after an adventure all my life, a pure dispassionate adventure, such as befell early and heroic voyagers, and thus to be found by morning in a random woodside nook in Gévaudan - not knowing north from south, as strange to my surroundings as the first man upon the earth, an inland castaway - was to find a fraction of my day-dreams realised.

For my part, I travel not to go anywhere, but to go. I travel for travel's sake. And to write about it afterwards, if only the public will be so condescending as to read. But the great affair is to move, to feel the needs and hitches of our life more nearly, to come down off this feather-bed of civilisation, and find the globe granite underfoot and strewn with cutting flints.

(Stevenson 1896)

'For my part,' wrote Stevenson the day before he walked through La Bastide, 'I travel not to go anywhere but to go, I travel for travel's sake.' The line is so well-worn that, like the mountaineers' aphorism 'Because it's there', it's almost lost its meaning. Stevenson's claim to fulfilment through aimlessness seemed to me a contradictory, impossible ideal. It wasn't till I read his journal that I realized he'd lopped off the end of this passage when he rewrote the text for TWAD. After 'I travel for travel's sake', he added in the original: 'And to write about it afterwards...'

(Crane 1997)

Authors have unintentionally persuaded simple men to suffer many blisters for the chance of drinking ale in the manner of Borrow and meeting adventures, in the hope of being heartily and Whitmanesquely democratic. A great many must be walking over England nowadays for the primary object of writing books: it has not been decided whether this is a worthy object.

(Edward Thomas 1913)

Roads

Perhaps if we walk long enough we shall discover something about roads. There could be few better objects for walking, unless it be to meet a mistress or to fetch a doctor. We walk for a thousand reasons, because we are tired of sitting, because we cannot rest, to get away from towns or to get into them, or because we cannot afford to ride, and for permanent use the last is perhaps the best, as it is the oldest.

(Edward Thomas 1913)

Roads are all more or less alike. Walking is intimate, it releases something unknown in any other form of travel and, arduous as it can be, the spring of the ground underfoot varies as much as the moods of the sky. By walking the whole way I got a sense of gradual transition from one place to another, a feeling of unity. The mosaic of my own country and its people had become a sensible pattern.

(Hillaby 1968)

Not only did I desire to follow a road most typical of all that roads have been for us in western Europe, but also to plunge right into the spirit of the oldest monument of the life men led on this island: I mean the oldest of which a continuous record remains [from Winchester to Canterbury].

For my part I desired to step exactly in the footprints of such ancestors. I believed that, as I followed their hesitations at the river-crossings, as I climbed where they had climbed to a shrine whence they had also seen a wide plain, as I suffered the fatigue they suffered, and laboriously chose, as they had chosen, the proper soils for going, something of their much keener life would wake again in the blood I drew from them, and that in a sort I should forget the vileness of my own time, and renew for some few days the better freedom of that vigorous morning when men were already erect, articulate, and worshipping God, but not yet broken by complexity and the long accumulation of evil.

(Belloc 1913)

I love to wander on these soft gentle mournful autumn days, alone among the quiet peaceful solitary meadows, tracing out the ancient footpaths and mossy overgrown stiles between farm and hamlet, village and town, musing of the many feet that have trodden these ancient and now well nigh deserted and almost forgotten ways and walking in the footsteps of the generations that have gone before and passed away.

(Kilvert, 31 August 1874)

Pilgrimage

[Hilaire Belloc makes a vow to walk from Toul to Rome]

I will start from the place where I served in arms for my sins, I will walk all the way and take advantage of no wheeled thing; I will sleep rough and cover thirty miles a day, and I will hear mass every morning, and I will be present at high mass in St. Peter's on the Feast of St. Peter and St. Paul.

(Belloc 1902)

[tramping along the Caucasian and Crimean shores of the Black Sea on a pilgrimage with seven thousand Russian peasants to Jerusalem]

It is the life of the wanderer and seeker, the walking hermit, the rebel against modern conditions and commercialism who has gone out into the wilderness.

One cannot make such a journey without great experiences both spiritual and material.

(Graham 1912)

The pilgrim is humble and devout, and human, and charitable, and ready to smile and admire, therefore he should comprehend the whole of his way, the people in it, and the hills and the clouds, and the habits of the various cities. And as to the method of doing this, we may go bicycling (though that is a little flurried) or driving (though that is luxurious and dangerous, because it brings us constantly against servants and flattery), but the best way of all is on foot, where one is a man like any other man, with the sky above one, and the road beneath, and the world on every side, and time to see all.

(Belloc 1906)

[On the road to Santiago]

I interrogated each pilgrim, filling my notebook with a census of the passing traffic, as if the sheer weight of collected detail would teach me how to make a walking journey and help me to understand my own motives. But no rules emerged from the accumulating data. None of the pilgrims had left home with the belief that hundreds of kilometres of hot hiking would really win them the promised remission of purgatory. Some however had experienced spiritual awakenings. Most were on holiday. The maddest were the ones who had walked the furthest, which was a worrying omen.

I met twenty or more a day. There were loners, lovers and losers. And there were families and friends, all moving west, one step at a time, dusty and sore. They looked like the earth's last evacuees, escaping along the only open road.

(Crane 1997)

You could tell which ones were pilgrims on their way to Santiago because they had scallop shells attached to their rucksacks ...

The most numerous were young Spaniards for whom the pilgrimage was obviously an impeccable excuse to get out of the parental home and meet other young Spaniards of the opposite sex...Then there were the more sophisticated young backpackers from other countries, bronzed and muscular, attracted by the buzz on the international grapevine that Santiago was a really cool trip, with great scenery, cheap wine and free space to spread your bedroll.

There were pilgrims with more particular and personal motives...People at turning-points in their lives -- looking for peace, or enlightenment, or just an escape from the daily rat-race. The pilgrims in this category were the ones who had travelled furthest, often walking all the way from their homes in northern Europe, camping on the way. Some had been on the road for months. Their faces were sunburned, their clothes weather-stained, and they had a kind of reserve or remoteness about them, as if they had acquired the habit of solitude on the long lonely miles, and found the somewhat boisterous and hearty company of other pilgrims unwelcome. Their eyes had a distant look, as though focussed on Santiago.

(Lodge 1995)

[a pilgrim]

Do not ask me the reasons why I am doing it. It is an adventure. To feel the vibrations of the stones under my feet, to prove I can do it. A lot of the people do not start as a pilgrim, but become one on the road. On the road, you open your mind, you get rid of your mental ballast and open yourself to other things ... in a full jar you can put nothing.

(Crane 1997)

You seem to drop out of time. You pay no attention to the news...All that matters are the basics: feeding yourself, not getting dehydrated, healing your blisters, getting to the next stopping-place before it gets too hot, or too cold, or too wet. Surviving. At first you think you'll go mad with loneliness and fatigue, but after a while you resent the presence of other people, you would rather walk on your own, be alone with your own thoughts, and the pain in your feet.

(Lodge 1995)

[on the road to Santiago with an old pilgrim and his son]

I began to suffer severe pains in my feet. At first I thought the cause was *anno Domini*, pampered living and lack of exercise, and that my Spartan pilgrim life would harden my feet. The pain, however, seemed to increase in intensity during my slow tramping with the two French pilgrims ... When I spoke of my sore feet to the bearded pilgrim he answered at once: "There is only one thing for you to do, go straightway to Lourdes. Your feet will be healed in the pool." ... A few minutes later when we saw a lorry approaching he stood in the middle of the road waving his arms. When the lorry stopped he told a wonderful sob-story about my feet and I was hoisted into the lorry beside the driver.

When I arrived in Lourdes my feet were hurting me so much that I could hardly walk, and the severity of the weather brought on continuous attacks of asthma and coughing ... one of the *brancardiers* who give devoted service to the sick asked me why I did not undergo the immersion in the *piscine*. So persuasive was he that I put myself in his hands. There were not many pilgrims about as there was an icy wind blowing and rain and sleet fell in torrents. When I was undressed he took a damp piece of navy blue cloth and wrapped it round me, and helped by him I descended into the bath, uttering all the time the ejaculations to Our Lady, which are printed upon a card hanging on the wall at the end of the bath. The water was desperately cold and made me gasp, but I had to lie back covered altogether by the water. The hospitaller then gave me a little silver statuette of Our Lady to hold in my hands and led me out of the bath. I then had to put on my clothes without drying my body, and thus shivering and clammy I went outside to face the rain and the sleet again. I felt at first strangely faint, but the hospitaller led me to a neighbouring hostel where I fell into a deep slumber. I awoke an hour later feeling strangely elated. I found to my amazement that I breathed freely and my feet no longer pained me. Such was my energy that I set off immediately to ascend the mountain *Via Crucis*, which is a mile in extent, saying the Stations of the Cross in thanks for my cure.

(Starkie 1957)

Therapeutic

[stumping along on a shoeful of blisters]

It seems to me now that my purely physical discomfort intensified the taste of the evening's beauty, as it certainly made sweeter the perfection of enjoyment which I imagine possible at such an hour and in such a place.

The road was serpentining very little, but enough to conceal from me for a long time the chief wayside marks ahead, as well as my destination. I could always see about a quarter of a mile before me, and there the white ribbon disappeared among trees. And this quarter-mile was agreeable in itself, and always suggesting something better beyond, though itself a sufficient end, if need were.

(Edward Thomas 1913)

I think that I cannot preserve my health and spirits unless I spend four hours a day at least - and it is commonly more than that - *sauntering* through the woods and over the hills and fields, absolutely free from all worldly engagements.

I, who cannot stay in my chamber for a single day without acquiring some rust, and when sometimes I have stolen forth for a walk at the eleventh hour of four o'clock in the afternoon, too late to redeem the day, when the shades of night were already beginning to be mingled with the daylight, have felt as if I had committed some sin to be atoned for. But the walking of which I speak has nothing in it akin to taking exercise, as it is called, as the sick take medicine at stated hours.

(Thoreau 1862)

It is injurious to the mind as well as to the body to be always in one place and always surrounded by the same circumstances ... I felt eager to escape from it ... there was a hill to which I used to resort at such periods. The labour of walking three miles to it, all the while gradually ascending, seemed to clear my blood of the heaviness accumulated at home. On a warm summer day the slow continued rise required continual effort, which carried away the sense of oppression. The familiar everyday scene was soon out of sight, I came to other trees, meadows, and fields, I began to breathe a new air and to have a fresher aspiration.

Moving up the sweet short turf, at every step my heart seemed to obtain a wider horizon of feeling, with every inhalation of rich pure air, a deeper desire. The very light of the sun was whiter and more brilliant here. By the time I had reached the summit I had entirely forgotten the petty circumstances and the annoyances of existence. I felt myself, myself.

(Jefferies 1883)

If Nature is to fertilize she must be given her chance to do her work. Hence, it is good that a man should be sometimes alone with Nature, with his senses open to country sights and sounds and his mind fallow, which means, of course, that he must be by himself, or at least in the company of one whom he knows so well that there is no need for the passing of words. But, even so, it is better that he should be alone.

One returns to the world of men and things, I will not say a better and a nicer person, but a calmer and a quieter, with a replenished fund of energy to tackle one's tasks and duties, and a new strength of serenity to bear one's crosses and distresses.

(Joad 1946)

In the days of those old walks I could have written a dedication in Norfolk-jacket style, all about "the open road," and the search for something "over the hills and far away".

Today I know there is nothing beyond the farthest of far ridges except a signpost to unknown places. The end is in the means - in the sight of that long straight line of the Downs in which a curve is latent. Today I know that I walk because it is necessary to do so in order both to live and to make a living.

(Edward Thomas 1913)

To Edward Thomas walking was not merely exercise, though he swung along with a long slow stride ... nor was he as he walked only the nature lover intent on observing birds and flowers and clouds ... nor was he only the aesthete satisfying his eye with the beauty of the contours of the hills, the symmetry of the trees, and the grouping of villages. Nor was he only the wayfarer meeting fellow-travellers on the roads and in the inns ... nor was he only the artist transmuting all this into words. He was all these and much more. By the English country his soul was revived when it was faint with despair, and comforted as some are by religion or music. There he could throw off his melancholy brooding and be content.

(Helen Thomas 1909)

There are times when a man must have a proper walk, at whatever cost, when his primary need is for 18 miles at 4 miles an hour, nay, there are times when he is simply not fit for company, and must go walking alone, and recapture something of himself before he can properly consort with his fellows.

This condition is called by many names in medical works, but there is a better and more expressive name, the Hump. The very word brings a clear vision of a definite deformity which he can attack and cure. Let him take a walk, and lo! the pressure is lightened, the Hump is reduced, and he resumes his natural shape.

(Sidgwick 1912)

I have two doctors, my left leg and my right. When body and mind are out of gear (and those twin parts of me live at such close quarters that the one always catches melancholy from the other) I know that I have only to call in my doctors and I shall be well again ... there are times when my thoughts, having been duly concentrated on the right spot, refuse to fire, and will think nothing except general misery ... on these occasions my recipe is to go for a long walk. My thoughts start out with me like bloodstained mutineers debauching themselves on board the ship they have captured, but I bring them home at nightfall, larking and tumbling over each other like happy little Boy Scouts at play, yet obedient to every order to "concentrate". That is, of course, a Sunday spent with both legs swinging all day over ground where grass or heather grows ... I never knew a man go for an honest day's walk, for whatever distance, great or small, his pair of compasses could measure out in the time, and not have his reward in the repossession of his own soul.

(Trevelyan 1913)

There is nothing you can do in your physical life which will not affect you for better or for worse as you walk. Walking is the book of the recording angel of the body, who never forgets or forgives. If you have sat up late, or eaten and drunk unwisely, or breathed foul air, or listened to or participated in waltzes, or done all these things simultaneously, which is quite easy - you will know it at the eighth mile next day. But if you have trained your body, and given it its due of food and drink and sun and air, then you will walk with a peculiar exaltation, you will swing your legs to the full rhythm of your physical being, you will feel yourself one with all the greatest moments of your bodily past.

(Sidgwick 1912)

Once in every man's youth there comes the hour when he must learn that the world was not created to make him happy. In such cases, grim Walking's the rule. Every man must once at least in life have the great vision of Earth as Hell. Then, while his soul within him is molten lava, let him set out and walk, whatever the weather, wherever he is, be it in the depths of London, and let him walk grimly, well if it be by night, to avoid the vulgar sights and face of men, appearing to him, in his then daemonic mood, as base beyond all endurance.

Let him walk until his flesh curse his spirit for driving it on, and his spirit spend its rage on his flesh in forcing it still pitilessly to sway the legs. Then the fire within him will not turn to soot and choke him, as it chokes those who linger at home with their grief ... The stricken one, as he plies his solitary pilgrimage day after day, finds that he has with him a companion with whom he is not ashamed to share his grief, even the Earth he treads, his mother who bore him. At the close of a well-trodden day grief can have strange visions and find mysterious comforts.

(Trevelyan 1913)

My strength is not enough to fulfill my desire. I have often walked the day long over the sward, and, compelled to pause, at length, in my weariness, I was full of the same eagerness with which I started. The sinews would obey no longer, but the will was the same. My frame could never take the violent exertion my heart demanded. Labour of body was the meat and drink to me. Over the open hills, up the steep ascents, mile after mile, there was deep enjoyment in the long-drawn breath, the spring of the foot, in the act of rapid movement. Never have I had enough of it, I wearied long before I was satisfied, and weariness did not bring cessation of desire, the thirst was still there.

(Jefferies 1883)

Meditation

Every day I walk myself into a state of well-being and walk away from every illness. I have walked myself into my best thoughts, and I know of no thought so burdensome that one cannot walk away from it. Thus if one keeps on walking, everything will be all right... I had been walking for an hour and a half and had done a great deal of thinking, and with the help of motion had really become a very agreeable person to myself.

(Kierkegaard 1847)

Walking is among recreations what ploughing and fishing are among industrial labours: it is primitive and simple, it brings us into contact with mother earth and unsophisticated nature, it requires no elaborate apparatus and no extraneous excitement. It is fit even for poets and philosophers, and he who can thoroughly enjoy it must have at least some capacity for worshipping the "cherub Contemplation". He must be able to enjoy his own society without the factitious stimulants of the more violent physical recreations ... the days when "muscular Christianity" was first preached and the whole duty of man said to consist in fearing God and walking a thousand miles in a thousand hours.

The true walker is one to whom the pursuit is in itself delightful, who is not indeed priggish enough to be above a certain complacency in the physical prowess required for his pursuit, but to whom the muscular effort of the legs is subsidiary to the "cerebration" stimulated by the effort, to the quiet musings and imaginings which arise most spontaneously as he walks, and generate the intellectual harmony which is the natural accompaniment to the monotonous tramp of his feet ... the true pedestrian loves walking because, so far from distracting his mind, it is favourable to the equable and abundant flow of tranquil and half-conscious meditation.

Perhaps, therefore, it is better to trust the case for walking to where the external stimulus of splendours and sublimities is not so overpowering. Walking gives a charm to the most commonplace British scenery. A love of walking not only makes any English county tolerable but seems to make the charm inexhaustible.

(Stephen 1901)

[Leslie Stephen]

He walked for no other reason than that the mere act of walking gave him pleasure. He did not walk because he wished to see celebrated views, or paint pictures, or write poetry, or examine glaciers, or study rocks, or watch birds, or explore new lands, or preach a gospel, or conquer a country, or pay a vow, or seek romance, or pursue Beauty - that will-o'- the-wisp, or any of the thousand and one reasons why men set out to walk. He was happy while he walked, whether the country chanced to be the Fens, the Lake District, the Cornish coast, or the shining snow peaks of the Alps.

(Murray 1939)

I can only meditate when I am walking. When I stop, I cease to think, my mind only works with my legs.

I do not remember ever having had in all my life a spell of time so completely free from care and anxiety as those seven or eight days spent on the road. Never did I think so much, exist so vividly, and experience so much, never have I been so much myself as in the journeys I have taken alone and on foot. There is something about walking which stimulates and enlivens my thoughts. When I stay in one place I can hardly think at all, my body has to be on the move to set my mind going. The sight of the countryside, the succession of pleasant views, the open air, a sound appetite, and the good health I gain by walking, the easy atmosphere of an inn, the absence of everything that makes me feel my dependence, of everything that recalls me to my situation - all these serve to free my spirit, to lend a greater boldness to my thinking, so that I can combine them, select them and make them mine as I will, without fear or restraint.

(Rousseau 1782)

The attainment of such a feeling requires a certain receptivity and even passivity of mind.

You cannot grasp the character of a country by a conscious effort of discursive reason, all you can do is to set your body fairly to its task, and to leave the intimate character of your surroundings to penetrate slowly into your higher faculties, aided by the consciousness of physical effort, the subtle rhythm of your walk, the feel of the earth beneath your feet, and the thousand intangible influences of sense. You must lay aside for the time being that formal and conscious reasoning which (you fondly think) gives you your distinctiveness and individuality in ordinary life, you must win back to deeper and commoner things, you must become mere man upon the face of your mother earth. Only in a state of humility and simplicity, with all views and arguments and chains of reasoning - all, in fact, that divides man from man - laid aside and utterly forsworn, can you enter the great democracy of walkers.

(Sidgwick 1912)

Some people, I am aware, think whilst they walk, and I have known of a case in which a newspaper leader was composed during an ascent of the Jungfrau. But, in my own case, which I take to be an ordinary one, the brain during active walking (and the result is one of the great charms of that form of exercise) becomes merely an instrument for co-ordinating the muscular energies. Enough thought is secreted to make legs and arms work harmoniously, and to propel the organism in any required direction, but there is no surplus of cerebration to take the shape of conscious intellectual effort. Vague phantoms of ideas may possibly flit across the brain, but they give rise at most to some vague simmering of the mind rather than to anything which can be called reasoning, or even meditation. Thought, that is, becomes indistinguishable from emotion. The outside world is not a collection of objects to be classified, and still less does it suggest trains of speculation, it is merely the background of a dream, its presence is felt rather than perceived, it is like the tapestry of some gorgeous chamber which one vaguely watches with half-shut eyes during the initial stages of a quiet doze. The mountains and the sky are potent influences, but if one attempts to analyse the specific elements which they contribute to thought, the charm would vanish.

Some people can enjoy such a frame of mind, when in a state of bodily inactivity. To me, I confess, this is very difficult. My body becomes a nuisance to me unless I provide it with occupation. For this reason, though a professed cultivator of the art of doing nothing, I find that even the seaside is not equal in sedative power to the mountains.

(Stephen 1901)

Into the hills

Why *does* a man climb mountains? Why has he forced his tired and sweating body up here when he might have instead been sitting at his ease in a deckchair at the seaside, looking at girls in bikinis, or fast asleep, or sucking ice-cream, according to his fancy? On the face of it the thing doesn't make sense.

Yet more and more people are turning to the hills, they find something in these wild places that can be found nowhere else. It may be solace for some, satisfaction for others: the joy of exercising muscles that modern ways of living have cramped, perhaps, or a balm for jangled nerves in the solitude and silence of the peaks, or escape from the clamour and tumult of everyday existence. It may have something to do with a man's subconscious search for beauty, growing keener as so much in the world grows uglier. It may be a need to re-adjust his sights, to get out of his own narrow groove and climb above it to see wider horizons and truer perspectives. In a few cases, it may even be a curiosity inspired by A Wainwright's *Pictorial Guides*. Or it may be, and for most walkers it will be, quite simply, a deep love of the hills, a love that has grown over the years, whatever motive first took them there: a feeling that these hills are friends, tried and trusted friends, always there when needed.

It is a question every man must answer for himself.

(Wainwright 1958)

... this urge which takes people to the hills. The urge defies analysis, but many of its components are within the range of ordinary human experience, as, for example, the attraction of beauty and unexpected strangeness which may lie round any corner on a mountain.

One may climb through dense mist and emerge above a sea of clouds stretching endlessly and unbroken to the horizon, or find a green translucent pool, warm as milk and made for bathing, among the rocks, or see a boulder-strewn hillside converted by the magic of mist into a petrified forest more terrible than the fears of childhood, yet friendly because it is understood.

(Borthwick 1939)

CHAPTER 3
WHERE DID YOU GO?

Places

The real meaning which places have for the walker is hard to analyse and impossible to define: in the last resort we are driven back on the metaphor of personal relations. There are places which are, so to speak, given to us from the beginning without our choice, like parents and family, places which are part of us and are not to be criticised or regarded from outside. There are places, on the other hand, like casual acquaintances which we choose for ourselves, which we see, and even see often, with pleasure, but with which we have little permanent intimacy. And there are places of a third kind, somewhere between the two former, which seem partly chosen by our conscious choice, partly given to us by a pre-ordained kinship, which may be viewed both from within and without, which have for us a special meaning and a special individuality. Whether the metaphor can be driven to a romantic-idealist conclusion, whether there is for everybody one especial place of the third type reserved for one unique intimacy, I would not venture to say.

(Sidgwick 1912)

Conversations about places are thus really like conversations about persons, and have all the charm and interest of this familiar conversational mode. We are interested when Jones has met our family acquaintances or friends, we are also interested when he has met our parent places (wherever they are), our acquaintance Helvellyn, or our very dear friend Bowfell. Did Jones merely visit Bowfell casually (via Esk Hause), or did he dine with him and converse until a late hour in the smoking-room (Hell Gill route)? Such talk is both lively and profitable, it brightens up both parties and speedily shows them whether they are destined for friendship or acquaintance. It may be that Jones is a mere trifler, who went up Bowfell as he would have gone up Skiddaw (that mountain of banality) and talked by the way, or tried to set up a record; if so, you may treat him kindly, but it is better to pass on to Wordsworth or politics or immortality or some more trivial subject. But it may prove that he is a real walker, of a reverent and concrete mind, and then you may get out your map and go over it with him, and talk about food and the weather.

(Sidgwick 1912)

London

And yet there is also a peculiar charm in the solitary expedition when your interlocutor must be yourself. That may be enjoyed, perhaps even best enjoyed, in London streets themselves. I am not sure that the roar of the Strand is not a more favourable environment than the quiet of my own study … though a London street is full of distractions, they become so multitudinous that they neutralise each other… A Cockney born and bred realises the common saying that the deepest solitude is solitude in a crowd, he derives a certain stimulus from a vague sympathy with the active life around him, but each particular stimulus remains, as the phrase goes, "below the threshold of consciousness." To some such effect, till psychologists will give me a better theory, I attribute the fact that what I please to call my "mind" seems to work more continuously and coherently in a street walk than elsewhere.

The charm is that even a walk in London often vaguely recalls better places and nobler forms of the exercise … little pictures of scenery, sometimes assignable to no definable place, start up invested with a faint aroma of old friendly walks and solitary meditations and strenuous exercise, and I feel convinced that, if I am not a thorough scoundrel, I owe that relative excellence to the harmless monomania of pedestrianism.

(Stephen 1901)

Give me the man that knows his bridges and has walked the whole range of all the embankments, from Blackfriars to the uttermost parts of Chelsea beneath the shadow of the four chimneys, he alone is the true Londoner.

The atmosphere of a town induces that dangerous combination of physical oppression and mental activity which leads to brilliant conversation: you shout epigrams across the roar of the traffic, and coruscate with wit as you dodge among perambulators. Town-walking in company tends to become like an evening party, and the only possible thing in a town is to walk alone.

The only thing to be done with most towns is to walk away from them as quickly as possible. But there is one exception, and that is London. London walking is a quite distinct and peculiar thing, utterly unlike any other town-walking.

If you walk London alone you will find that you approach most nearly to pure rusticity: there are so many people in London that they do not notice each other so that, for practical purposes, they are not there: the men are simply as trees walking. The difference between walking along Oxford Street and along the Embankment is only the difference between walking through a copse where there are many trees or on a field track where there are few. You can wear what you please, no one will notice or criticise. Even more important, you can sing in the streets. The roar of the traffic will drown all but the strongest passages in the highest register: and even if this lulls for a moment nobody will notice.

The mere size of London comes to the solitary walker's aid. It is large enough to give him the feeling of direction, to feed his craving for big lines. By walking in this way it is possible to gain some real idea of London. The greatest and most inspiring thing is the river, with the morning sun catching it as one drops on to the embankment from the north, the silver mornings when the air is clear, the gold mornings with a slight fog, and the copper mornings with a thicker fog.

(Sidgwick 1912)

The zig-zag walk

Did you ever make one? Probably not, for it is my secret. I invented it - a haphazard tramp, a setting out to walk without the name of any place you want to get to - the zig-zag walk. Keep taking the first turning on the left and the next on the right, and see where it leads you. In towns this gives you a most alluring adventure. But in the country you get tied up in a hopeless tangle of lanes which go back upon themselves.

The first turning to the left is the way of the heart. Take it at random and you are sure to find something pleasant and diverting. Take the left again and the piquancy may be repeated. But reason must come to the rescue, and you must turn to the right in order to save yourself from a mere uninteresting circle.

(Graham 1927)

∗∗∗

But urban wanderings, delicious as they are, are not quite what we mean by walking. On pavements one goes by fit and start, halting to see, to hear, and to speculate. In the country one captures the true ecstasy of the long, unbroken swing, the harmonious glow of mind and body, eyes fed, soul feasted, brain and muscle exercised alike.

(Morley 1918)

A bright hot sun and cold east wind, the sky a deep and wonderful blue and the roads dry. Teddy [brother] and I decided to go up today to Overton on the Marlborough Downs. We went by train to Calne at ten o'clock.

In the presence of the great silent White Horse on the hillside at Cherhill we turned into the Black Horse for some ale. Then on and over the long white road stretching up and down but rising ever across the backs of the great rolling downs, with the sun glaring hot and scorching on our right hand and the N.E. wind piercing keen on our left.

Soon we came in sight of the first outlying barrow rising over a shoulder of the down, solemn, mysterious, holding its secret in unbroken silence and impenetrable mystery. There was a ceaseless singing of larks in the vast empty expanse of the sky and down. They were rising in the sunshine all over the hills. The monotony of the downs was broken here and there by spinneys and scattered lonely clumps of trees, chiefly fir and beech. Teams of horses and oxen were crawling slowly along the great slopes at plough and harrow, and one team of four white oxen harrowing in the distance seemed scarcely to move at all. The grey tower of Yatesbury Church rose among the grove of trees which sheltered the village, far on the left. The keen wind hummed a melancholy song among the telegraph wires and each post had its own peculiar measure and mournful song. Solitary barrows rose here and there upon the heaving down.

The sun glared blinding upon the white flint road and the white chalk land, and the great yellow dandelions by the road side stared at the sun. On, on, up the interminable road winding like a white ribbon over the green downs till at length we climbed to 'Needle Point', the highest ridge, and began to descend towards Beckhampton. As we got between hedges once more the banks were snowy with black thorn blossom and the country was filled with the bleating of flocks.

Then the King of the Barrows, strange, vast, mysterious Silbury Hill came in sight, the great problem, the world's puzzle, with the white chalk landslip on its steep lofty green slope. The great cloud shadows came flying over the downs and sweeping swiftly across the Mount. At Kennet our eyes were refreshed by the vivid green of the rich low water meadows and the soft murmur of the streams, and our hearts by the thought of the strong Kennet ale that we should get at Overton.

Along the crest of the last ascent, Seven Barrows Hill, the five remaining barrows rose in a line marking perhaps the graves of an army that had been destroyed in defending the old Roman road. The road avoids Silbury Hill and makes a detour round it, showing that the hill is older than the road. This fact has been proved by excavation. In harvest time the line of this Roman road may be distinctly traced, for the wheat growing along the line of the road is ripe some days earlier than anywhere else on the down.

(Kilvert 15 April 1874)

Plains

It is all flat and all dull. I believe there are some pleasant tracks in it, and on a fine day if you had just become engaged to be married, had been made Poet Laureate, and been give ten thousand a year, it might be enjoyable. But in a north-east wind, under a sombre sky and rain, in the dead period of the afternoon, I found it dull.

(Sidgwick 1918b)

At this tranquil hour of the evening, when not a living being seemed to stir, an overpowering feeling of loneliness descends upon the solitary wanderer. Wandering in the mountains never induces loneliness, because they limit the flight of the human spirit, but in the plain that loses itself in the blue horizon there is infinity. In the mountains I hear church bells resounding in the valleys, and there is comfort in the distant sounds of village life, but in the never-ending plain, discouragement dogs the wanderer who longs to see hills in the distance, for they make him think of the spires and towers of cities. Probably this feeling of melancholy which I experienced was due to weeks of wandering in the plains, for the people who dwell in plains are never merry.

(Starkie 1933) [on the plains of Hungary]

The line of the mountains rose higher against the sky, and there entered into my pilgrimage for the first time the loneliness and the mystery of meres. Something of what a man feels in East England belonged to this last of the plain under the guardian hills.

Everywhere I passed ponds and reeds, and saw the level streaks of sunset reflected in stagnant waters ... my whole spirit was caught or lifted in the influence of the waste waters and of the birds of evening.

(Belloc 1902) [on the border of France and Switzerland]

East Anglia

I used to climb the range of the Gogmagogs, to see the tower of Ely, some sixteen miles across the dead level, and I boasted that every term I devised a new route for walking to the cathedral from Cambridge... the charm was in the distance "from anywhere" - a sense of solitude under the great canopy of the heavens.

I have always loved walks in the Fens. In a steady march along one of the great dykes by the monotonous canal with the exuberant vegetation dozing in its stagnant waters, we were imbibing the spirit of the scenery ... the absence, perhaps, of definite barriers makes you realise that you are on the surface of a planet rolling through free and boundless space.

(Stephen 1901)

The East Anglian is not in general a good countryside for walking. There is not enough detail in the immediate foreground and as a result little feeling of intimacy. The scene changes but slowly and there is not, therefore, enough sense of variety. Walking in East Anglia is in fact a little like walking on the Continent. For cycling and even motoring the eastern counties are superb, the scenery changes rapidly enough to occupy the eye and the lovely skylines especially in Essex make the employment of the eye a delight.

The eastern sky, huger, nobler and somehow more eventful, can be seen on a bicycle as well as, perhaps better than it can be seen on foot. You top the rise and see before you an apparently endless expanse of unemphatic, undulating country. There is no distinction, no focal point, no climax, just another rise in the far distance beyond which you know there will spread another similar expanse. All this, agreeable enough to cyclist and motorist, is apt to be depressing to the slow-going walker.

(Joad 1946)

Rivers

There is a strange and wonderful vigilance about the river which rolls past us where we sleep in the grass, murmuring and calling the whole night long, something of the vigilance of the starry sky. You sleep, but an eternal sleepless sentry paces by all the while.

(Graham 1927)

For company I chose one of the most enchanting little streams in Cornwall, the head-water of the River Fowey. The rivulet ran ahead of me for hours, prattling away about nothing in particular and agreeing with whatever I thought about. I like company of this kind.

(Hillaby 1968)

As we walked along the edge of the lake for miles and miles, it occurred to me that although a lake is not such a good conversationalist as, say, a brook or a river, it had eloquent silences which were wholly to my liking.

(Hillaby 1964)

[Thoreau] invented what he called the fluvial walk. Taking off his trousers and wrapping his shirt about him like a toga, he waded along the beds of rivers. This, he thought, was the ideal summer walking. There was always a current of air above the stream, as well as the flowing water, which made it the easiest highway ... a stream was a road where no dust was ever known and no intolerable drought. His feet could expand on the smooth sandy bottom or contract timidly on the pebbles, slump in what to him was 'genial fatty mud'.

(Murray 1939)

Bridges

No properly constituted man ever crosses a bridge without pausing. He must at least lean on the parapet on one side and look at the water, and then lean on the parapet on the other side and look at the water. Some bridges are specially made for the purpose, with piers jutting out, and an angle at the top of each on which to lean. Scientific people will tell you that the object of these is to break the force of the current, but I know better. They are made to look nice, and to lean upon.

(Sidgwick 1918b)

Forest

I climbed through the mist on to a verdant mountainside spread beneath a sky of purest blue. Streams tumbled down terraced slopes, a cuckoo called, and my track unravelled through woods of oak, birch and sweet chestnut. In places the trees closed above my head so that I felt as if I was walking underwater, through a long, thin, sun-filled aquarium. That night I lay down under an oak and slept too deeply to dream.

(Crane 1997)

Rain begins as I set out and mount under the beeches. The sky is dark as a ploughed field, but the leaves overhead are full of light like precious stones. The rain keeps the eyes down so that they see one by one the little things of the wayside.

(Edward Thomas 1909)

As I gained the darkness of the first trees, rain was falling.

The silence of the interior wood was enhanced by a rare drip of water from the boughs that stood out straight and tangled I know not how far above me. Its gloom was rendered more tremendous by the half-light and lowering of the sky which the ceiling of branches concealed. Height, stillness, and a sort of expectancy controlled the memories of the place, and I passed silently and lightly between the high columns of the trees from night (as it seemed) through a kind of twilight forward to a near night beyond … Had not the trees been so much greater and more enduring than my own presence, I should have felt afraid. As it was I pushed upward through their immovable host in some such catching of the breath as men have when they walk at night straining for a sound, and I felt myself to be continually in a hidden companionship.

(Belloc 1902)

Walking up the peaty valley-side pathway under the tall trees, in the shade, looking out through the trees at the sunshine, the wide view, glimpses of Marburg Castle, the blue sky. On my own, taking my time, aged 20, I felt an intensely uplifting sense of the hugeness and beauty and wonder of the world, and felt that I could do *anything* I wanted, such a feeling of being part of it all, having my place in it all, and an optimism and exuberance of possibilities and my own energy and power, almost a sacred moment, magical, and so empowering, such a surge of happiness, awe, delight.

Judith Bartlett (May 1990)

The conifers gave way to straggly oak and beech that made a high-pitched breathing noise in the rain. This is a peculiarity of deciduous forests. During a downpour, coniferous woods are strangely silent. The needles are wonderful insulators of sound, but among broad leaves you are aware of the squalls, for the rise and fall of the gusts sound like a long-drawn-out sigh.

(Hillaby 1972)

The going is like nothing on earth because your feet are not on the ground. Densed-in by soundless spruce, you tread a nether soil of fibrous droppings, in a close-canopy plantation that destroys all flora by shading them from the sun and then by stifling them with needle-leaves. In summer the forest resembles an ill-lit Turkish bath, in winter, a cistern with a tendency to leak.

(Peel 1972) [in Wark Forest]

Near the house, high on a hill, were woods of pine and fir, and, slipping away from the others, I followed a path that led me into one of these woods, through a tunnel of green gloom and smoky blue dusk. It was very quiet, very remote in there. My feet sank into the pile of the pine needles. The last bright tatters of sunlight vanished. Some bird went whirring and left behind a deeper silence. I breathed a different air, ancient and aromatic. I had not gone a hundred paces before I had walked out of our English South-country and was deep in the Northern forest itself, with a thickness of time, centuries and centuries of it, pressing against me. Little doors at the back of my mind were softly opened. It was not the mere quickening of fancy that brought me delight then, but an atavistic stirring and heightening of the imagination, as if all my distant ancestors, who were certainly of the North, were whispering and pointing in this sudden dusk. Any turn now might bring me to the magical smithy, the cave of the dragon, a horn might blow and shatter the present time like so much painted glass, the world of legend, hung about these trees like the spiders' webs, was closing round me. No doubt my precious ego, challenged at every step, felt a touch of fear! But my true self, recognising this enlargement of life, finding its place for a moment or two in that procession which is the real life of Man, drew deeper breaths, lived in its own world during those moments, and was delighted.

(Priestley 1951b)

Downs

It has been debated and cannot be resolved, why these great lines of chalk north and south of the Weald achieve an impression of majesty. They are not very high. Their outline is monotonous and their surface bare. Something of that economy and reserve by whose power the classic in verse or architecture grows upon the mind is present in the Downs. Those which we had travelled that day were not my own hills ... but they were similar because they stood up above the sand and the pines, and because they were of that white barren soil, clothed in close turf, wherein nothing but the beech, the yew, and our own affection can take root and grow.

(Belloc 1913)

The top of a down always gives a lift to your spirits. Its wide convexity feels as if it must be the spherical swell of the whole globe. Poised high on the great ball, you seem to look commandingly down on all its gently rounded slopes.

(Montague 1924)

... a wide empty land [the Downs]. That emptiness seemed good for the mind and body, and I could spend long hours idly *sauntering* or sitting and lying on the turf ... thinking of nothing, or only of one thing - that it was a relief to have no thought about anything.

(Hudson, *'A shepherd's life'*, in Peel 1984)

For my part, I find such ridge walking [South Downs] dull and monotonous. Views seen and wondered at are not really looked at again, there are few flowers and birds on this northern ridge, and the immediate foreground lacks variety. Presently one begins to feel that one is walking for exercise.

(Joad 1946)

I found my track at length, and going along the side of a field I experienced a quite sudden and unaccountable elevation of spirits.

I hope that other people who walk will know what I mean. Quite apart from the definite and sustained stretches of glory which come to us all at times, there are occasional spurts of exaltation, born of the minute and often perishing in the minute, emphatically in the aorist tense, dependent on no external circumstances, but just bubbling up spontaneously out of the inner consciousness. At such a moment you do not sing or gesticulate: you simply fling back your head, add an extra two inches to your stride, and wonder why you were ever unhappy.

... a true Surrey track, strong and beautiful, satisfying to the soul. It turned southward and began to mount, soon fields opened out ahead, not niggling little patches of arable land maintaining a precarious life under the shadow of encroachment, but great expanses rising up in big lines to the ridge ahead. It was the chalk at last, the stuff out of which is carved the main structure of the South of England, the material in which the sculptor made no mistake.

(Sidgwick 1918b)

It was late, and the day was already falling when I came, sitting my horse Monster, to a rise of land. We were at a walk, for we had gone very far since early morning, and were now off the turf upon the hard road, moreover, the hill, though gentle, had been prolonged. From its summit I saw before me, as I had seen it a hundred times, the whole of the weald.

But now that landscape was transfigured, because many influences had met to make it, for the moment, an enchanted land. The autumn, coming late, had crowded it with colours, a slight mist drew out the distances, and along the horizon stood out, quite even and grey like mountains, the solemn presence of the Downs. Over all this the sky was full of storm.

In some manner which language cannot express, and hardly music, the vision was unearthly. All the lesser heights of the plain ministered to one effect, a picture which was to other pictures what the marvellous is to the experience of common things. The distant mills, the edges of heath and the pine trees, were as though they had not before been caught by the eyes of travellers, and would not, after the brief space of their apparition, be seen again. Here was a countryside whose every outline was familiar, and yet it was pervaded by a general quality of the uplifted and the strange. And for that one hour under the sunset the county did not seem to me a thing well known, but rather adored.

The glow of evening, which had seemed to put this horizon into another place and time than ours, warned me of darkness, and I made off the road to the right for an inn that I knew of, that stands close to the upper Arun and is very good.

(Belloc 1906)

A good road is recognised as the groundwork of civilisation. So long as there is a firm and artificial track under his feet the traveller may be said to be in contact with city and town, no matter how far they may be distant ... some of our own highways winding through Down districts are bounded by undisturbed soil. Such a road wears for itself a hollow, and the bank at the top is fringed with long rough grass ... grasping this as a handle to climb up by, the explorer finds a rising slope of sward, and having walked over the first ridge, shutting off the road behind him, is at once out of civilisation. There is no noise. Wherever there are men there is a hum, even in the harvest-field, but here the long, long slopes, the endless ridges, the gaps between, hazy and indistinct, are absolutely without noise.

Glance along the slope, up the ridge, across the next, endeavour to penetrate the hazy gap, but no one is visible. In reality it is not quite so vacant, there may, perhaps, be four or five men between this spot and the gap, which would be a pass if the Downs were high enough.

By walking a mile the explorer may, perhaps, sight one of these ... and when you have walked the mile - knowing the distance by the time occupied in traversing it - if you look back you will sigh at the hopelessness of getting over the hills. The mile is such a little way, only just along one slope and down into the narrow valley strewn with flints and small boulders. If that is a mile, it must be another up to the white chalk quarry yonder, another to the copse on the ridge, and how far is the hazy horizon where the ridges crowd on and hide each other? Like rowing at sea, you row and row and row, and seem where you started - waves in front and waves behind, so you may walk and walk and walk, and still there is the entrenchment on the summit, at the foot of which, well in sight, you were resting some hours ago.

(Jefferies 1909)

[walking with D. H. Lawrence]

In the spring of 1915 ... I decided to walk across the Downs, keeping as much as I could to the Roman Way. Lawrence said he would do the first day's walk to Chichester with me. We were making an early start, and met at the gate in one of those white Sussex mists which muffle the meadows before sunrise, lying breast-high on the earth, her last dream before waking. We set out, then, in a world still asleep, the known lanes and fields were strangers, as friends sleeping become strangers. The woolly haystacks and the sheep huddled against them were not yet actual haystacks and real sheep. They were still being dreamed by the land. If a lamb had bleated, one felt the dream must break, earth stir in her bed, and shake the sleep out of her eyes. We talked in lowered voices. At that time I walked with a long lope that matched Edward Thomas's negligent stride. He covered ground fast without any appearance of hurry. It was too fast for Lawrence, who soon said, "I must teach you to walk like a tramp. When you are going to walk all day you must learn to amble and rest every mile or so." We padded it gently to the foot of the Downs, walking rather as though we were tired at the end of the day than fresh at the start of it. The low-lying sun began to melt the mists as we climbed, unpacking the world from its lamb's-wool. Soon all that was left of the mist was a sparkle of dew on the grass.

Lawrence was in an angelic mood, almost child-like. We found, followed, and lost the old track the Romans had made over the Downs to Chichester. We lost ourselves as well as the track, and wandered among curling valleys that led us astray. We only occasionally looked at the map. We sang scraps of songs, and every two miles lolled on the grass, where, till the dew had dried, I spread my green silk mackintosh. It was a new one, and Lawrence approved of it. We ate snacks from my knapsack, and talked when we felt like it ... In one of the deep bottoms, where the whitebeams looked like trees in silver blossom, he cried,

"We must be springlike!" and broke green branches and stuck them round our hats.

The day turned extremely hot, more June than April. In the afternoon the food I had brought was exhausted. We became thirsty, and were still lost in the hills. At teatime when we took our rest we drowsed. Thirst grew intolerable, high among the Downs, far from the smell of a pub. When we rose to go on our way, "Shandygaff!" cried Lawrence, and as we walked began to complain to the world, "I want my shandygaff!"...The next inn was all we cared about in the world. Suddenly I halted.

"My belt!"

"Eh?"

"I've left the belt of my mackintosh where we lay down."

He eyed me. The resting-place was at least a mile behind us.

I said, "It is a brand-new mackintosh."

"I like it best without a belt," said Lawrence.

(Farjeon 1941)

The Ridgeway

In China and the East there were no doubt older roads, but most of these have been buried in sand, whilst the kindly turf of our climate has formed a protecting covering to the Ridgeway, till now perhaps it can claim to be actually the oldest road in the world ...

Much is, and must be, guesswork, since all the evidence that remains to guide us, are the trackways and earthworks ... The accepted explanation that the earthworks were tribal strongholds, used for local purposes only, appears to me impossible to maintain after examining a map of the watersheds. These hill forts are obviously arranged systematically along the watersheds, and there is much evidence to prove that they were connected together by a fully developed system of travel-ways...

Along these trackways a system of contour forts follow the lines of hills from end to end ... these forts are seldom more than a day's journey, or ten to twelve miles apart ... when protected with more than one tier of ramparts and ditches they are admirably placed for defence, but when surrounded by a single bank and ditch the position is usually less suggestive of defence, and it is not unlikely that such secondary camps served as cattle compounds to the larger fortresses...

The evidence, though mostly exclusive, points to the Stone Age as the period when the hill forts were built, and if the ridge roads can be attributed to the same time it follows that a civilization existed in this country long before the Celtic invasions.

(Cox 1914)

The use [of a road] as a military way involved a feature not accidental or probable, but necessary, and this feature was a number of stations the distance between which should correspond to a day's march, and in which the troops should rest at the end of each stage...now, an average day's march for a considerable force is a matter of from 12 to 13 miles. The comparative shortness of this distance may surprise the reader. Men are, of course, capable of very much more...but when there is no occasion for haste, the average set here will be found to agree most nearly with experience.

(Belloc 1913)

Nearly all the original trackways follow the dry ridges, and in particular the chalk. One may say, with slight exaggeration, that the chalk was the essential factor in the building up of British communications before the Roman civilization came ... it has two characters which give it this character. In the first place, it is self-drained and always passable even in our wettest seasons, and, in the second place, it does not carry tangled undergrowth, and even its woods (which are not as a rule continuous) are commonly of beech - the easiest of all woods to pass through in travel, from the absence of scrub beneath the branches.

(Belloc 1924)

These Downs provide some of the finest walking in England. Less strenuous than the trackways of the Pennines and Cheviots, less steep and water-crossed than Offa's Dyke, softer and kinder to the feet than the oolitic belt of Dorset and Cotswolds, these Downs offer bracing air, magnificent panoramas, dry and firm footing and, perhaps above all, the constant visual reminder that here our forbears lived.

(Hogg 1946)

The internet of drove roads, coffin roads and sunken lanes has undoubtedly shrunk but some remain and there is a sentimental pleasure in hearing in the sound of your footsteps the echo of those that have passed before.

(Wilson 1998)

Hedges no longer bounded either side of the broad turf track. It was as free as the blue paths in the snowy heavens. It looked down upon everything but the clouds, and not seldom on them in the early morning or in rain.

Now the Ridgeway had risen up to its perfect freedom, away from the river and the low land, from the glaring roads and the collections of houses. This way men of old came of necessity, yet I found it hard not to think now that the road was thus climbing to heights of speculation, to places suited for exploring the ridges and solitudes of the spirit, it seemed in one mood a hermit road going out into the wilderness to meditate and be in lifelong retirement, in another mood a road for the young, eager warrior or reformer going up and away for a time from cloying companions to renew his mighty youth.

I saw, however, more racehorses than confirmed hermits or aspiring warriors or reformers.

(Edward Thomas 1913)

Leaving Goring on a wet autumn afternoon some years ago I took the Ridgeway to Avebury, crossed the Vale of Pewsey, and turned west on Salisbury Plain, following the line of hill forts as Cox had done. By the fifth afternoon I had reached Cadbury Castle, the object of this pilgrimage. The next day I walked off the map and into Sherborne.

On the way back I miscalculated and arrived in a small town after dark in fine rain, tired, dirty and very hungry. The notice outside the hotel announced that dinner was now being served. The hall and lounge were empty. Dropping my rucksack behind a sofa, I squelched down the passage. The dining-room was empty except for a couple - obviously Madame and her husband - who were being served by a waiter. I said that I would like to book a room, have a bath, dinner and a bottle of something special. Madame looked me in the eye - without a glance at my distressing trousers and unmentionable boots - and said she was sorry, but they were absolutely packed out.

Outside it was now raining hard, and across the road was the triangular sign of a Youth Hostel. I hadn't been inside one for thirty-five years. The lady warden was charming. When I asked if she could suggest somewhere for me to stay as I had foolishly arrived late without booking a room she asked why I didn't stay in the Hostel. I said I wasn't a member, but she said it didn't matter as it was raining and I couldn't go on that night. She apologized for not giving me a room to myself, as an unexpected school party had just arrived, but she put me in a room with one other man, saying 'I hope you will be comfortable'.

(Patterson 1977)

[In September 1913, for his last term at school, Charles Sorley walked from his home in Cambridge to Marlborough]

The walk was most successful after the first day. After ten miles of towpath, interesting at first from the number of gaudy barges with spitting men that passed up the canal with loads of sand, but after a little very irritating, I struck west for the Icknield Way and spent the rest of the day making bad shots at short cuts till in the end I was glad to get to Princes Risboro, almost entirely by road. But the next two days were much better. I struck the Icknield Way, and, except for a few miles in the Thames valley, was on grass for the rest of the way. My progress at first was very slow owing to the abundance of brambles by the side of it, but, after crossing the Thames and leaving Bucks for Berks where vegetation gave place to downs, I got on much faster and soon came into a land well-known to me from memories of past field-days. About this time the sky grew very black behind me and I raced the rain to East Ilsley and arrived a few minutes in front of it.

The last day was the best of all. Almost all the time I was seven or eight hundred feet up, for I was walking on the ridge that forms the southern wall of the White Horse Vale, and all the time had a fine panorama to my right. The early morning was thick with mist, but cleared up wonderfully later on. There was a track all the way, sufficiently visible to follow, and I kept it till the ridge breaks off due south of Swindon. Then I turned at right angles on to the top of that other ridge that runs east by the road from Swindon to Marlborough, and separates Wilts and Berks, and on its back I threaded my way back to College. When once I had arrived there, it rained for the rest of the night. So altogether I was in very good luck.

(Sorley 1913)

[on the Icknield Way in the Chilterns]

The Chilterns are beautiful at all seasons, but in spring and autumn they surpass themselves, so that the October tints and the April leaves take even a native by surprise. I chose to travel in spring, during the first week of May, when the young foliage adds a gloss to Richard Jefferies' maxim: 'Beech and beautiful scenery go together.' Imagine, therefore, a green road climbing gently among beech trees, with hills ahead and hills astern, and on your right a vale whose destination is the horizon ... I once met a man who had tried three times to follow this sector, but never got above a quarter of a mile from the foot of Wain Hill, not because of the gradient, but because of the birds and the sun and the beeches. Having walked a few hundred yards, he became so enchanted that he sat down on a mossy bank, feeling that he was in Paradise, and need proceed no further.

(Peel 1976)

Stonehenge

I perceived what I at first conceived to be a small grove of blighted trunks of oaks, barked and grey ... as I drew nearer, I perceived that the objects which had attracted my curiosity, and which formed a kind of circle, were not trees, but immense upright stones.

A thrill pervaded my system, just before me were two, the mightiest of the whole, tall as the stems of proud oaks, supporting on their tops a huge transverse stone, and forming a wonderful doorway. I knew now where I was, and, laying down my stick and bundle, and taking off my hat, I advanced slowly, and cast myself - it was folly, perhaps, but I could not help what I did - cast myself, with my face on the dewy earth, in the middle of the portal of giants, beneath the transverse stone.

The spirit of Stonehenge was strong upon me!

(Borrow 1851)

How did these same "few old stones" strike me on a first visit? It was one of the greatest disillusionments I ever experienced. Stonehenge looked small - pitiably small! As a child I had stood in imagination before it, gazing up awestruck on those stupendous stones and crawling like a small beetle on them. And what at last did I see with my physical eyes? Was this Stonehenge - this cluster of poor little grey stones, looking in the distance like a small flock of sheep or goats grazing on that immense down! It was only when I had recovered from the first shock, when I had got to the very place and stood among the stones, that I began to experience something of the feeling appropriate to the occasion.

The feeling, however, must have been very slight, since it permitted me to become interested in the appearance and actions of a few sparrows inhabiting the temple.

(Hudson 1909)

Today I paid my first visit to Stonehenge. We had breakfast before Church and immediately after service Morris and I started to walk to Stonehenge, eleven miles ... we took the Devizes road and after we had walked along that road for some six miles we saw in the dim distance the mysterious Stones standing upon the Plain.

The sun was hot, but a sweet soft air moved over the Plain, 'wafting' the scent of the purple heather tufts and the beds of thyme and making the delicate blue harebells tremble on their fragile stems. A beautiful little wheatear flitted before us from one stone heap to another along the side of the wheel track as we struck across the firm elastic turf. Around us the Plain heaved mournfully with great and solemn barrows, the 'grassy barrows of the happier dead'. It seemed to be holy ground and the very Acre of God ... across the turf eastward we came in sight of the grey cluster of gigantic Stones.

They stood in the midst of a green plain, and the first impression they left on my mind was that of a group of people standing about and talking together. It seemed to me as if they were ancient giants who suddenly became silent and stiffened into stone directly anyone approached, but who might at any moment become alive again, and at certain seasons, as at midnight and on Old Christmas and Midsummers Eve, might form a true 'Chorea Gigantum' and circle on the plain in a solemn and stately dance

It was a solemn awful place. As I entered the charmed circle of the sombre Stones I instinctively uncovered my head. It was like entering a great Cathedral Church. A great silent service was going on and the Stones inaudibly whispered to each other the grand secret. The Sun was present at the service in his Temple and the place was filled with his glory. During the service we sat under the shadow of the great leaning stone upon the vast monolith which has fallen upon and crushed and which now nearly covers the Hearth or Altar Stone. Many Stones still stood upright, one leaned forward towards the East, as if bowing to the rising sun, while some had fallen flat on their faces as if prostrate before the Lamp of Heaven, or as if like Dagon they had fallen across the threshold of the Temple before the advent of a purer faith, and in reluctant acknowledgment and worship of One Greater than They.

It must be a solemn thing to pass a night among the silent shadows of the awful Stones, to see the Sun leave his Temple in the evening with a farewell smile, and to watch for him again until at morning he enters once more by the great Eastern gate and takes his seat upon the altar stone.

As we went down the southern slope of the green plain we left the Stones standing on the hill against the sky, seeming by turns to be the Enchanted Giants, the Silent Preachers, the Sleepless Watchers, the great Cathedral on the Plain.

(Kilvert 27 August 1875)

Offa's Dyke

The Dyke is the most unusual of Britain's long-distance footpaths, officially opened in 1971. It is unique as a walk in that it follows a man-made monument, not a natural line, such as a coast or range of hills.

(Hunter Davies 1982)

The Welsh border, on both sides of it, is good ground. If you would walk away for a while out of modern England, back and away for twice two hundred years, arrange so that a long day's tramping may drop you at nightfall off the Black Mountain on to the inn that nestles in the ruined tower of old Llanthony. Then go on through

Clunton and Clunbury, Clungunford and Clun,

The quietest places under the sun.

Follow more or less the line of Offa's Dyke, which passes, a disregarded bank, through the remotest loveliness of gorse-covered down and thick, trailing vegetation of the valley bottoms.

(Trevelyan 1913)

Moors

At some evening twilight, or morning of mist, you leave roads behind first, and then tracks, and strike into the open moor as a ship goes into the pathless Atlantic at night. Almost at once you are reposefully simplified, all that is complicated and inessential about you peels itself off, coat by coat, till, behold! nothing is left but a body as fit as your past may have made it, an eye to read a map and compass and watch, a brain to connect what you read, and a will to go on in absolute faith in those three.

(Montague 1924)

I reached the top of the ridge just as the sun went down. For the last half-hour I had been walking through heather, and now it was all around me, stretching as far as I could see, and giving rich colour to the rolling moorland. But it was not the heather alone that held me entranced. As the sun vanished, the sky was cleared of clouds as though a huge magic broom had swept them away, overhead, and down to the wide horizon, was a vast canopy of purest blue. In all the heavens there was not a speck to mar the wonderful colouring. I might have walked through the stratosphere and looked for the first time into infinite space. Around me, and far into the distance, the hills were etched crystal-clear, and landmarks stood out prominently, in bold relief, giving a stereoscopic effect so unusual as to be almost startling. The valleys below me were hidden in an impenetrable white mist, as if they were stuffed with cotton wool, a pure unstained white, solid and yet soft, it seemed that I could have walked from my present position right across the vale of Blanchland to the moors beyond and sink no further than ankle-deep in the white clinging mass. These then were the colours: blue, purple, and white, there were no others.

The evening was still, there was not a sound to disturb the tranquillity of the peaceful scene. I saw it alone ... I alone was privileged, and I was a man made conscious of his soul.

(Wainwright 1986)

Yorkshire Dales

A feature of the Yorkshire Dales country is the network of 'green' roads (i.e. grass-covered) crossing the hills and linking the valleys: relic of the days when trade was carried on by the use of horse transport. Where these routes run along the valleys they have long been superseded by tarmac roads, but motors have not been able to follow the horses over the hills and the high moorland ways have fallen into disuse, they are, however, still plain to see and joy to walk upon, being well-graded and sufficiently distinct on the ground to remove doubts of route-finding. Often they are walled on one or both sides, sometimes they run free and unfettered across the breasts of the hills and over the skyline. For pedestrian exercise these old packhorse roads are excellent: quiet and traffic-free they lead effortlessly into and over the hills amid wild and lonely scenery, green ribbons threading their way through bog and heather and rushes. They call a man to go with them.

(Wainwright 1966)

Penyghent

I proceeded at a snail's pace up the green track, faithfully adhering to all its zig-zags. The more strenuous short cuts were beyond me, I was very, very tired ... I was in poor condition. The hills demand a high standard of fitness in a man before they admit him to their company. That first day, I had no right to be there, and they treated me with scant respect.

After struggling upwards for more than an hour, the gradient eased and I was well satisfied to be atop the ridge ... the view was superb: in that moment when I turned and surveyed the way I had come, my lethargy was shaken off as though I had discarded a wearisome cloak.

The sun had disappeared only a few minutes before, and Penyghent, dark and shadowy, reared up like a great purple wedge in the molten sky. There was no disputing its majesty... a noble peak that so arrested my attention as to make me forget my tiredness and hunger, and set my heart singing again.

I lingered awhile, I was very conscious of being utterly alone amongst the silent hills. I would recover from my exertions in a few hours, but the reward I found on that Sabbath evening will remain with me as long as I live. It was one of the unforgettable moments.

(Wainwright 1986)

Peak District

I am not an enthusiast for the Peak District. It is wild, it is even grand, but the grandeur partakes of the savage rather than of the beautiful. All the ingredients which make the north of England so attractive to the southerner are present, hills and rocks, heather-clad moorlands, swift rushing streams of clear water, wide views, above all, the sense of space and remoteness. For this is big country, it is austere, almost scornful in its disdain for the adventitious prettinesses of flower and coppice and hedgerow. It can be formidable, too, to be lost in a mist on Kinder Scout and put to the necessity of dropping into and climbing out of the deep peat ditches with which the top of that gloomy plateau is seamed and scarred is no joke, while the outcropping rocks of blackened gritstone, grim enough at all times, when the mist comes down and the rain falls look very forbidding indeed.

(Joad 1946)

[Samuel Johnson in Derbyshire]

Ilam excels Dovedale by the extent of its prospects, the awfulness of its shades, the horrors of its precipices, the verdure of its hollows, and the loftiness of its rocks. The ideas which it forces upon the mind are the sublime, the dreadful, and the vast. Above is inaccessible altitude, below is horrible profundity ... He that mounts the precipices wonders how he came thither, and doubts how he shall return. His walk is an adventure, and his departure an escape.

(Marples 1959)

Northumberland

Alpine or Cumbrian mountains, from their very height and the nearness of one giant to another, hide the wealth of heaven from the climber on the hillside, who has, however, in those lands his terrestrial compensations. In fen country the clouds are seen, but at the price of an earth of flat disillusionment. In Northumberland alone both heaven and earth are seen, we walk all day on long ridges, high enough to give far views of moor and valley, and the sense of solitude above the world below, yet so far distant from each other, and of such equal height, that we can watch the low skirting clouds as they "post o'er land and ocean without rest". It is the land of the far horizons, where the piled or drifted shapes of gathered vapour are for ever moving along the farthest ridge of hills, like the procession of long primaeval ages that is written in tribal mounds and Roman camps and Border towers on the breast of Northumberland.

For the distance, the illimitable, is seldom out of sight. The far ridge, the horizon rich with cloud shapes, is always there. Like all the greatest things, like the universe itself, this land does not easily yield up the truth, whether its secret heart is of joy or of sorrow. It heightens both till they are fused, and the dispute between them loses meaning. The great silence is too profound to be broken with a question. The distance is so grand that we cannot wish it near. We are satisfied by we know not what.

(Trevelyan 1913)

Pennines

The formative ridge of the Pennine is dropped half-way down the country southwards like the firmer cartilage in the flesh of a widening nose.

(Montague 1924)

PENNINES IN APRIL

If this county were a sea (that is solid rock

Deeper than any sea) these hills heaving

Out of the east, mass behind mass, at this height

Hoisting heather and stones to the sky

Must burst upwards and topple into Lancashire

Perhaps, as the earth turns, such ground-stresses

Do come rolling westward through the locked land.

Now, measuring the miles of silence

Your eye takes the strain: through

Landscapes gliding blue as water

Those barrellings of strength are heaving slowly and heave

To your feet and surf upwards

In a still, fiery air, hauling the imagination,

Carrying the larks upward.

(Ted Hughes 1960)

At the station they left the main valley and walked for two hours up a tributary defile. It narrowed and blackened till both its sides were steep slants of dark shale, with the solid rock cropping out from it in low vertical tiers of crag, each with its own refuse-shoot of broken stone streaming away from its foot. The sides converged at last to form a rough gulley of scree. Up it the three walkers stumbled and puffed, to emerge above on the upper storey of Northern England ... An hour's wading through heather and bilberries led them out on to a plateau a little higher still. It was springy ground, barer now, and peat-dark ... [they] finally came to a stand at a boss or tussock of peat, perhaps a yard square and rising a couple of feet above the bed of the eroded trenches that reticulated the whole surface of the moss.

'Top of England - this hummock.'

'Not, of course, the very highest point.'

'No, no disrespect to Scawfell. But the ridge of the roof.'

From the flooded outer cells at one side of the soaked sponge the brown bog-water oozed out and trickled a few inches down its outer wall ... in the bed of the trench at its foot there was enough water moving to break on a stone in its way with an infinitesimal plash, the first cry of an infant river.

'The Mersey!'

Across the hummock on its far side there welled slow drop after drop into a lower reach of the trench. There was more water there, it had other feeders, at the far end if moved away visibly.

'If you might call the other the Mersey, then perhaps you might call this the Trent!'

'Jump on the hummock, all jump. Make a flood in the German Ocean and Irish Sea.

Inundate Liverpool and Hull!'

(Montague 1913)

The Pennine Way

Presently the mist cleared, the rain stopped, and I saw the full desolation of treeless bog speckled with heather and gorse, an utter absence of human life, no bird-song, no flower, not even a sheep. And all this was something more than an aesthetic impression, it was an aspect of the essence of the Way, and one to be examined more closely, for it confirmed that I had entered the north of England.

(Peel 1972)

If the Pennine Way passed through unchanging scenery it would be a treadmill. But its main appeal is variety. You pass, day after day, into fresh scenes, new worlds of enquiry. They should not be entered or left in a hurry. You may not come this way again.

(Wainwright 1968)

For life is nowhere more itself, its hardy, invincible self, than on the crown of the Pennine. There the land lies black for mile after mile of soaked bog, just endless hummocks of peat, the whole waste reticulated and sluggishly drained by ditch-like depressions which moat each hummock off from the rest and receive the sullen brown oozings from its saturated tissues. The place, if you give it only a summary glance, may seem morose, lethargic, dead. Looked at more closely it becomes the scene of endless gallant or stoic contrivance, the dodges and shifts of unbeaten stickers to life.

(Montague 1924)

The Pennine Way is masculine, the Coast to Coast Walk has feminine characteristics. If there happens to be something in your temperament that makes you like the ladies the odds are that you will prefer the C. to C. You may not meet any but you will be reminded of them. On the PW you never give them a thought ... well, hardly ever.

(Wainwright 1973)

... the summit of Black Hill, which I take to be the most desolate spot in all the Way, and the most dangerous. I came here only once, and that will last my lifetime. Through heavy rain I came, when the sky grazed the land in mutual animosity. Dampness, dourness, drudgery, desolation, that was how humanity translated the scene. If there were any trees, I did not notice them, neither did I observe any bird, beast, or creeping thing that might have ventured out on such a day in such a place.

The summit is called Soldiers' Lump because of the military surveys that have been made from it ... to reach it you must wade through the black bog which baptized the place. In that bog I went up to my knees, which means down to my knees, trying to discover where they were, and when at last I did discover them, I got what I believe is called the Hell out of it.

(Peel 1972)

A local saying from which I derived no comfort is that if you can see Cross Fell (the highest point on the Pennine Way) it's going to rain and if you can't it is raining.

(Hillaby 1968)

Anyone who has climbed Cross Fell will understand why the ancients believed that it really was haunted by evil spirits. Even modern science allows that there is much turbulence on the Fell, though its fiendishness is nowadays called the Helm Wind, which bowls over hikers and hayricks and horses. Even in calm weather the wind on Cross Fell is seldom still...

(Peel 1972)

[from *Pennine Way Companion*: arrangements have been made with the Border Hotel at Kirk Yetholm for *bona fide* Pennine Wayfarers *who have completed the walk in a single journey* to be supplied with a congratulatory pint (of beer or lemonade, NOT whisky - and, one only, mind you!) at the author's expense. Just say "Charge it to Wainwright." Cheers! (P.S. You'd better have some money of your own, in case his credit has run out).]

2 April 1974

Dear Mr Wainwright,

You must receive many appreciative letters from walkers, but I would like to be one of the first this year to thank you for the very welcome pint at the Border Hotel last night.

As I could not get anyone to come with me at this time of year, I was particularly grateful for your skilful guidance in some tricky situations and your good-humoured companionship at all times [*Pennine Way Companion*].

Yours sincerely,

Tom Patterson

6 April 1974

Dear Mr Patterson

You are very welcome to the pint, and well earned it. In fact, being a bit cynical about the Pennine Way (believing there is much better walking to be found elsewhere in this fair country of ours), I consider that anyone who walks the Pennine Way from end to end and lives to tell the tale, deserves shares in a brewery.

Yours sincerely,

A. Wainwright

[on Hadrian's Wall]

The wind was strong on the top and every time I reached a summit it suddenly tore at my ears and into my skull. Yet down in the hollows everything was still, eerily still, so that I began to imagine I could hear voices, people talking round the next crag. When I got to the top again, and was met by a howl of wind, I could see nobody. Once again, I could sympathise with Romans and anyone for that matter believing in local deities and spirits. When you're alone for any time on the heights of the Wall you begin to think you might even be a spirit yourself, invincible and ethereal, able to throw yourself off over Crag Lough and just float to the heavens.

(Hunter Davies 1993)

Coast

The voice of the sea is as powerful as the voice of the mountain ... the solitude of the frozen peaks suggests tombstones and death. The sea is always alive and at work.

Of all the walks that I have made, I can remember none more delightful than those round the south-west promontory ... from the mouth of the Bristol Avon by the Land's End to the Isle of Wight, and I am only puzzled to decide which bay or cape is the most delightful.

(Stephen 1901)

We had waited throughout one long rainy day for a chance of finer weather before we started to explore the Lizard promontory. But our patience availed us little. The next morning, there was the soft, thick, misty Cornish rain still falling, just as it had already done without cessation for twenty-four hours. To wait longer, in perfect inactivity, was beyond mortal endurance. We shouldered our knapsacks, and started for the Lizard in defiance of rain, and in defiance of our landlady's reiterated assertions that we should lose our way in the mist, and should slip into invisible holes, and fall over fog-veiled precipices among the rocks.

What sort of scenery we walked through, I am unable to say. The rain was above - the mud was below - the mist was all around us ... a good-humoured peasant informed us with a grin, that this sort of 'fine rain' often lasted for a fortnight.

(Wilkie Collins 1851)

I wandered round the cliffs to the broken rocks at the furthest point of Gurnard's Head, and sat alone amongst the wilderness of broken shattered tumbled cliffs, listening to the booming and breaking of the waves below and watching the flying skirts of the showers of spray. Perfect solitude. The rest of the party were climbing about in the rocks somewhere overhead, but not a voice or sound was to be heard except the boom of the sea and the crying of the white-winged gulls. Not a sigh or vestige of any other living thing.

(Kilvert 29 July 1870)

The rambles I have described were mostly inland, when by chance they took us down to the sea, our impressions and adventures appeared less interesting. Looking back on the holiday, it would seem to us somewhat vacant time compared to one spent wandering from village to village. I mean if we do not take into account that first impression which the sea invariably makes on us on returning to it after a long absence - the shock of recognition and wonder and joy, as if we had been suffering from loss of memory and it had now suddenly come back to us. That brief moving experience over, there is little the sea can give us to compare with the land.

(Hudson 1909)

My lukewarmness in regard to coast walking is the comparative bareness of coasts. The fields are few and infertile and the crops poor. Even in September blackberries tend to be dry and stunted. Except where the sea birds gather, there are few birds and apart from the occasional rabbit, no beasts. I tire of the view, on one side always the sea, on the other a hedge maybe or a field or a wall, but rarely an expanse. Finally, when it comes to walking, you can walk only in three instead of four directions which is, I suppose, one of the reasons why walking by the sea always seems limited.

(Joad 1946)

When you have made an early start, followed the coastguard track on the slopes above the cliffs, struggled through the gold and purple carpeting of gorse and heather on the moors, dipped down into quaint little coves with a primitive fishing village, followed the blinding whiteness of the sands round a lonely bay, and at last emerged upon a headland where you can settle into a nook of the rocks, look down upon the glorious blue of the Atlantic waves breaking into foam on the granite, and see the distant sea-levels glimmering away till they blend imperceptibly into cloudland, then you can consume your modest sandwiches, light your pipe, and feel more virtuous and thoroughly at peace with the universe than it is easy even to conceive yourself elsewhere. I have fancied myself on such occasions a felicitous blend of poet and saint - which is an agreeable sensation. What I wish to point out, however, is that the sensation is confined to the walker.

(Stephen 1901)

But I note that he [Leslie Stephen] used to walk there in the summer, when the heather was "purple". I prefer Easter for that region, because when spring comes to deliver our island, like the Prince of Orange, he lands first in the south-west. That is when the gorse first smells warm on the clifftop ... when the heather is "purple" I will look for it elsewhere.

(Trevelyan 1913)

Passes

There was no bad wine in one's youth, and even today there is not such a thing as a bad mountain pass. The mere descent from one were joy enough to fill holidays - the easing of your breath, the flagging stride set suddenly free, the road that has begun to bear you of itself, as moving staircases do, down its unwinding coils, miles and miles of them on ahead, lying like tumbled white tape thrown on a floor, rising and falling, it seems to the eye, capriciously.

But the sharpest delight of all attends the last stage of the rise. The surprise that your effort has earned is about to be paid you. The savour of contrast that all passes possess has matured: it awaits your absorption, not half a mile off. As you near the top, you feel that things are astir as if with some delicate sense of approaching events, cool air begins to lip over, it goes to your head, you exult to be reaching one of the spots where the make of the earth, its adventures and workings, come to a point and show themselves in their cunning variety and coherence.

... the window is suddenly opened, the air comes blowing through, there is a thrill as of a curtain rising or of a chapter begun. You need no telling that here, where the cutting makes its sharper nick at the bottom of a gentle dip of the sky-line, there have, in all ages since man ceased to walk on all-fours, been considerable leapings of the heart and drawings of deep breaths.

(Montague 1924)

Mountain passes have a way of accumulating mystique. They are places of battles with weather and between men. They mark borders. They are places of redemption (who has not crossed a high pass and thanked God?), they are places to rest or to die.

(Crane 1997)

I was soon amongst the desolate hills, which then looked more desolate than they did from a distance. They were of a wretched russet colour ... and if there was here nothing to cheer the eye there was nothing to cheer the ear. There were no songs of birds, no voices of rills...

I went on slowly and heavily, at length I got to the top of this wretched range - then what a sudden change! Beautiful hills in the far east, a fair valley below me, and groves and woods on each side of the road which led down to it. The sight filled my veins with fresh life, and I descended this side of the hill as merrily as I had come up the other side despondingly.

(Borrow 1862)

Since, in crossing a range, it is usually possible to find a low point suitable for surmounting it, such summit roads are rare, but when one does get them they are the finest travel in the world, for they furnish at one point (that is, at the summit) what ordinary roads going through passes can never give you: a moment of domination. From their climax you look over the whole world, and you feel your journey to be adventurous and your advance to have taken some great definite step from one province and people to another.

(Belloc 1902)

Ecstasy, I know, is an unfashionable commodity. At points on the trip when I slept out under the stars or got through the hills by means of gaps as spectacular as you can find anywhere, I can only say it was a privilege to be there.

(Hillaby 1968)

One Summer morning I lifted up a bank from a river to a village … the bank on which the village stood above that river had behind it a solemn slope of woodland leading up gently to where, two miles or more away, yet not three hundred feet above me, the new green of the tree-tops made a line along the sky. Clouds of a little, happy, hurrying sort ran across the gentle blue of that heaven, and I thought, as I went onward into the forest upland, that I had come to very good things: but indeed I had come to things of a graver kind.

A path went on athwart the woods and upwards. This path was first regular, and then grew less and less marked … the height was lonely when I reached it, as though it were engaged in a sort of contemplation … men had not often come that way, and those men only the few of the countryside.

Just where the slope began to go downwards again on the further side, the wood closed in again. The path wholly failed, and I had now to push my way through many twigs and interlacing brambles, till in a little while that forest ceased abruptly upon the edge of a falling sward, and I saw before me the Valley.

Upon the western bank grew a thick growth of low chestnuts with here and there a tall silver birch standing up among them. All this further slope was so held, and the chestnuts made a dark belt from which the tall graces of the birches lifted. The sunlight was behind that long afternoon of hills.

Opposite, the higher eastern slope stood full though gentle to the glorious light, and it was all a rise of pasture land. Its crest showed here and there a brown rock, aged and strong and half covered in the grass. These rocks were warm and mellow. This eastern boundary was not so high as to carry any sense of savagery. It warned rather than forbade the approach of human kind. Between it and its opposing wooded fellow the narrowing floor of that Eden lay: winding, closing slowly, until it ended in a little cup-like pass, an easy saddle of grass. The sun was shining on all this: it made upon the little cup-like place a gentle shadow and a gentle light, both curved as the light might fall low and aslant upon a wooden bowl clothed in a soft green cloth. This was a lovely sight, and it invited me to go forward. The valley was a wonder to me there.

It was not as are common and earthly things. There was a peace about it which was not a mere repose, but rather something active which invited and intrigued. The meadows had a summons in them, and all was completely still. I heard no birds from the moment when I left the woodland, but a little brook, not shallow, ran past me for a companion as I went on. Never have I found a place so much its own master and so contentedly alone.

Here was a place in which thought settled upon itself, and was not concerned with unanswerable things, and here was a place in which memory did not trouble one with the incompletion of recent trial, but rather stretched back to things so very old that all sense of evil had been well purged out of them. The ultimate age of the world which is also its youth, was here securely preserved. I was not so foolish as to attempt a prolongation of this blessedness: these things are not for possession: they are an earnest only of things which we may perhaps possess, but not while the business is on.

So I went on until I came to the low pass, and when I had surmounted it I looked down a steep great fall into quite another land. I had come to a line where met two provinces, two different kinds of men, and this second valley was the end of one.

The moor (for so I would call it) upon the further side fell away and away distantly, till at its foot it struck a plain whereon I could see, further and further off to a very distant horizon, cities and fields and the anxious life of men.

(Belloc 1912 b)

CHAPTER 4

WHAT WAS IT LIKE IN THE HILLS?

The difference between a hill and a mountain depends on *appearance*, not on *altitude* (whatever learned authorities may say to the contrary) and is thus arbitrary and a matter of personal opinion. Grass predominates on a hill, rock on a mountain. A hill is smooth, a mountain rough.

(Wainwright 1958)

In most parts of the world, sacred meanings are ascribed to mountains, and though the spirit world may be terrifying, it is seldom evil. Christian Europe seems to be alone in having seen mountains as ugly and almost hellish realms.

(Solnit 2001)

The wild Highlanders have loved their rugged mountains ... but those mountains were, until the latter part of the Eighteenth Century, a horror to the lowlander and above all to the Englishman.

One of the causes of the dislike felt by civilized man in those days [was] the lively fear of the fate that was apt to befall him amid their recesses.

But today we have learnt to love the Highlands and the snowy Alps also. There has been a change in aesthetic appreciation - our tastes are wider, we still love the woodland and hedgerow, but we also love the black rugged line of rocks on the skyline.

(Trevelyan 1949)

It has seemed to me that lovers of nature can be divided into two classes. The first desire to lose themselves in nature, they like wide views and big spaces, mountains and moorlands and great bare fields, they like, the more sophisticated of them, flat fenland country, where the sky is the chief feature and where, sensing their own insignificance in the vast prospect, they may forget the nervous little clod of wants and ailments which is the self, by absorption in something greater than the self.

The second class go to nature not to forget but to realize themselves, their desire is that their personalities shall be enhanced not absorbed. Accordingly, they seek not large scenery but small, not downs and open spaces but wooded dells and glades, copses, lanes and meadows, the courses of little streams, of narrow valleys running up into the hills.

Mountains they like but for their lower levels, eschewing heights which make them feel insignificant and therefore uncomfortable.

(Joad 1932)

It is well to seek as much variety as possible in twelve hours. Road and track, field and wood, mountain, hill and plain should follow each other in shifting vision ...the districts along the foot of mountain ranges are often the most varied in feature, and therefore the best for Walking.

(Trevelyan 1913)

Men of all ages have looked at mountains and have interpreted them in the light of their own social and religious needs ... Philosophers have looked and have meditated, then they have pronounced upon them. But behind their pronouncements the mountains stand still smiling and inscrutable. We will mean for you what you wish, they seem to say. What we really are, you can never know.

For the Buddhist through contemplation, of a mountain for instance, the idea of self can be lost and there is hope of entering Nirvana or the divine nothingness. 'But the western mind', Leslie Stephen has written, 'refuses to lend itself long to such uncongenial efforts.

Thoughts of dinner ...' He 'climbed because he liked it', and if he could not discover the reason why he liked it, then he did not fret.

His grandchildren are those who in their thousands flood the mountain area nearest to their home. In them has been born almost a new mysticism ... this no longer demands things from mountains, but is content to accept the experience as satisfying and allow it to lead them where it will.

(Noyce 1950)

If I were to invent a new idolatry (rather a needless task) I should prostrate myself, not before beast, or ocean, or sun, but before one of those gigantic masses to which, in spite of all reason, it is impossible not to attribute some shadowy personality. Their voice is mystic and has found discordant interpreters, but to me at least it speaks in tones at once more tender and more awe-inspiring than that of any mortal teacher.

(Stephen 1894)

A man may be more deeply affected by a feeling for mountain scenery than by any other kind of experience, and he will only find full satisfaction as long as he had access to the objects of his desire...

Yet if he is a normal being, he will be unable to live contentedly with the contemplation of scenery as a sole preoccupation, so that he seems to be impelled to link himself physically and mentally by means of some material activity to the environment that he needs...

The action, mental or physical, may involve him in the forlorn hope of somehow recording the vision of the glory that for an instant has appeared to him unveiled, or it may launch him on the lifelong pilgrimage of the mountaineer.

So if we are to discover a meaning in the lover-like attitude to mountains it is not the pretext on the surface that calls for investigation, but the underlying urge, the longing for perfection, which is the strongest of the motives that can lure us to the hills, and may be said to be mystical in its character...

Probably most people have at some time or other had some sort of mystical experience, if only of a rudimentary kind. Very likely they have been scarcely aware of it, or they may have been unwilling to confess to it if it did not come within the scope of their philosophy...

In fact, if the mountain-lover is not too reticent he can show that the mysterious quality is a state of mind that is shared by all mystics in varying degrees and possesses certain easily recognised characteristics. Among these is an acute sense of well-being beyond the reach of logic, bringing with it a profound conviction that all is well with the world, and giving a feeling of kinship with the whole of creation, as if the seeker and the object sought were about to be absorbed in an all-embracing unity.

(Meade 1954)

Something happens to you in the silent places which never could in the towns, and it is a good thing to sit awhile in a quiet spot and meditate. The hills have a power to soothe and heal which is their very own. No man ever sat alone on the top of a hill and planned a murder or a robbery, and no man ever came down from the hills without feeling in some way refreshed, and the better for his experience.

(Wainwright 1986)

And of these emotions the strongest, perhaps, is that which most of those who travel to-day go seeking, the enchantment of mountains: the air by which we know them for something utterly different from high hills. Accustomed to the contour of downs and tors, or to the valleys and long slopes that introduce a range, we come to some wider horizon and see, far off, a further line of hills. To hills all the mind is attuned: a moderate ecstasy. The clouds are above the hills, lying level in the empty sky, men and their ploughs have visited, it seems, all the land about us. Till, suddenly, faint but hard, a cloud less varied, a greyer portion of the infinite sky itself, is seen to be permanent above the world. Then all our grasp of the wide view breaks down. We change. The valleys and the tiny towns, the unseen mites of men, the gleams or threads of roads, are prostrate, covering a little watching space before the shrine of this dominant and towering presence.

It is as though humanity were permitted to break through the vulgar illusion of daily sense, and to learn in a physical experience how unreal are all the absolute standards by which we build. It is as though the vast and the unexpected had a purpose, and that purpose were the showing to mankind in rare glimpses what places are designed for the soul - those ultimate places where things common become shadows and fail, and the one divine part in us, which adores and desires, breathes its own air, and is at last alive.

(Belloc 1906)

Nature, no doubt, can fortify and console even in southern woodlands and on smooth hillsides. But to many of us the moorland and the mountain seem to have more rugged power and faithfulness, with which in solitude we can converse and draw thence strength and comfort. And the mountain above all seems to have personality, which says to us as we gaze on it at evening from the valley-head below - 'I know, I understand. Such is the lot of man. I have watched him through the ages. But there is a secret behind. It will always be a secret.' That at least is what the mountains say to me when they talk. To others they may say something different. But to many they have something important to say, whatever it may be. If this personality of mountains is a fallacy, it is none the less a potent and beneficent emotion. It is one of the ways by which men see God. It is one of the sacraments prepared for man, or discovered by man.

(Trevelyan 1949)

And this is a peculiar thing I have noticed in all mountains, and have never been able to understand - namely, that if you draw a plan or section to scale, your mountain does not seem a very important thing. One should not, in theory, be able to dominate from its height, nor to feel the world small below one, nor to hold the whole countryside in one's hand - yet one does. The mountains from their heights reveal to us two truths. They suddenly make us feel our insignificance, and at the same time they free the immortal Mind, and let it feel its greatness, and they release it from the earth.

(Belloc 1902)

Oddly enough, that desire which we all have at times for wings, or at all events for the power of flight, and which, like other vague and idle promptings, is capable of cultivation and of being made a real source of pleasure, most often comes to me on these great green hills. Here are no inviting woods and mysterious green shades that ask to be explored, they stand naked to the sky, and on them the mind becomes more aërial, less conscious of gravity and a too solid body. Standing on one great green hill, and looking across vast intervening hollows to other round heights and hills beyond and far away, the wish is more than a wish, and I can almost realise the sensation of being other than I am - a creature with the instinct of flight and the correlated faculty, that in a little while, when I have gazed my full and am ready to change my place, I shall lift great heron-like wings and fly with little effort to other points of view.

(Hudson 1899)

[on a mountain at the Gateway of Castile]

When I climbed up the mountain I was obeying a deep impulse within me. At certain periods of our life we long to stop the inexorable ticking hand of time and meditate upon our whole destiny. But alas, in the turmoil of today it is well-nigh impossible to drop out of the line and halt a while...

My greatest joy in my wandering springs from my sensation of silent solitude ... when I wander away from my world, I am free to converse with my different personalities and I even allow each of them a little freedom of expression from time to time.

I wanted to reach the domain of silence in the upper air and purify myself after my life in the plain ... in this kingdom of silence I can make my examination of conscience. When I look back on my days of wandering, I feel a sense of profound melancholy as though the scenes I had witnessed, the fugitive melodies I had heard, the personalities I had met for a fleeting instant were all part of a vague dream. When I was following my humble life as a vagabond minstrel in the villages I lived for the moment without a thought for the morrow. Up here in my present melancholy mood, with the sun sinking behind the mountain on the horizon, I feel a sense of helplessness in face of the cruel universe...

During the long period before the sunrise I had felt a sense of oppression as though the air was heavy with dew. Then all of a sudden there came a slight rustling breeze as if somebody had opened a window in the sky to purify the earth and brush away the cobwebs of the night ... all my pessimistic thoughts of the night fled as though by enchantment, and I was eager to continue my wandering through the plain.

(Starkie 1934)

A stranger in a mountainous country may not be aware that his walk in the early morning ought to be taken on the eastern side of the vale, otherwise he will lose the morning light, first touching the tops and thence creeping down the sides of the opposite hills, as the sun ascends, or he may go to some central eminence, commanding both the shadows from the eastern and the lights upon the western mountains. But, if the horizon line in the east be low, the western side may be taken for the sake of the reflections, upon the water, of light from the rising sun. In the evening, for like reasons, the contrary course should be taken.

(Wordsworth 1835)

There is only one way to know a hill, and that is to put your feet on it and walk. Wander about leisurely if you wish, but better still, make the summit your objective and struggle up to it. Plunge into the bracken and heather, and wrestle with the thousand tentacles that would hold you back, splash through the streams that silver the hillside, scramble up the rocks and know the thrill that enslaves the mountaineer, sweat and pant, slip and tumble, and curse if you are so minded, and rest often. But get to the top. And if up there you find a gale so strong as to bowl you off your feet, or you are privileged to be in the nerve-centre of a thunderstorm, so much the better. Stay on the summit as long as you may, then come down. Don't tread circumspectly now, but run, run as if all the fiends of hell were loose at your heels. Run with giant strides, leap, jump, tumble and sprawl and roll, come down helter-skelter until you reach the level ground in the valley. Wash in the stream, and bathe your wounds, and clean yourself up a bit. Then seek out a royal feed and a soft bed..... If you have done all this, one of two things has happened to you. Either you will never want to see a hill again, in which case you may safely assume that the rot has settled in your soul so deeply that nothing will remove it, or you will hunger for the next opportunity, do it again and again, and keep young for ever.

(Wainwright 1986)

Wales

The next day I started for Merthyr, which was only four miles distant [from Aberdare].

However, it was the worst four miles I had ever walked in all my life. Not because it was two miles up a steep mountain, and two miles down the other side, but because of the roughness of the road and there being no fine scenery. And going down was worse than going up, for when I got into Merthyr I was so shaken by the last two miles that I could feel every part of my inside, my heart was beating, stitches were in my sides, a blister burned my heel [he had only one leg], and something was gnawing at the pit of my stomach. I could now well understand the reason why the Welsh people hated walking, and rode to every place over a couple of miles from where they lived.

(Davies 1918)

[on a tumulus on the Black Mountain]

Imagine my delight to find the place perfectly silent and solitary except for the sheep. It was so much grander to visit the old-world resting place of the wild warriors alone in the silence of the summer afternoon with no-one to look on but the great mountains than to be stunned by the prattle of the Woolhope Club, or to be disgusted by the sight of a herd of Hay holiday-makers and sight-seers cutting bad jokes and playing the fool or straddling and dancing upon the grave. It is a fine thing to be out on the hills alone. A man can hardly be a beast or a fool alone on a great mountain. There is no company like the grand solemn beautiful hills. They fascinate and grow upon us and one has the feeling and love for them which one has for nothing else.

(Kilvert 1871)

[on the Black Mountains]

Leaving the road we struck off to the left over some rough ground, banks and gullies and we struck a track with hoof marks winding up the steep mountain side, and soon we were at the top, which was covered with peat bog and black and yellow coarse rushy grass and reed. Here and there were pools and holes filled with black peaty waters. The ground was frozen hard and icy-snow lay in the hollows and long icicles dripped from stones and little rock caves in the hillside. The mountains were very silent and desolate. No human being in sight, not a tree. No living thing moved except a few mountain sheep, some of them with long curling horns. Not a bird to be heard or seen. The only sounds were the sighing of the wind through the rushes and the rushing of distant streams in the watercourses with which the mountain sides were seamed and scarred. We tumbled about on the flat tableland of the mountain top over the rush tumps and tufts and among the treacherous holes and pools, and presently came in sight of the Vale of Ewyas, into which we plunged down the steep mountain side arriving soon at the foot among small rushy meadows, very swampy, enclosed by wire fences.

(Kilvert 9 March 1870)

[on the Prescelly Hills]

The track became so narrow that I decided I was following a sheep-path. This did not worry me, because the day was still young, and in any event I had deliberately chosen to wander on the summit of Prescelly Top, which the Welsh call Foel Cwm-cerwyn, nearly eighteen hundred feet above Saint George's Channel. Not a cloud marred the sky. Not a building blocked the vista of turf and gorse and drystone walls. High overhead, a conclave of larks were glad to be alive, and said so, in their own lyrical language. Nothing else was audible until I moved, and then a breeze uttered its own tone of voice, scarcely loud enough to bend a grassblade.

(Peel 1984)

[on Plynlimmon]

A mountainous wilderness extended on every side, a waste of russet-coloured hills, with here and there a black craggy summit. No signs of life or cultivation were to be discovered, and the eye might search in vain for a grove or even a single tree.

"This does not seem to be a country of much society," said I to my guide.

"It is not, sir ... Plunlummon is not a sociable country, sir, nothing to be found in it, but here and there a few sheep, or a shepherd."

I looked down, and saw far below what appeared to be part of a small sheet of water.

"And that is the source of the Rheidol?" said I.

"Yes, sir," said my guide, "that is the flynnon of the Rheidol."

"Well," said I, "is there no getting to it?"

"Oh, yes! but the path, sir, as you see, is rather steep and dangerous."

"Never mind," said I. "Let us try it."

"Isn't seeing the fountain sufficient for you, sir?"

"By no means," said I. "It is not only necessary for me to see the sources of the rivers, but to drink of them, in order that in after times I may be able to harangue about them with a tone of confidence and authority."

"Then follow me, sir, but please to take care, for this path is more fit for sheep or shepherds than gentlefolk."

And a truly bad path I found it, so bad indeed that before I had descended twenty yards, I almost repented having ventured. I had a capital guide, however, who went before and told me where to plant my steps ... after kneeling down and drinking freely of the lake, I said: - "Now, where are we to go to next?"

[he is taken to the source of the Severn]

... a little pool of water some twenty inches long, six wide, and about three deep ... after taking possession of the Severn by drinking at its source, rather a shabby source for so noble a stream, I said, "Now let us go to the fountain of the Wye."

"And now I suppose, sir, that our work is done, and we may go back to where we came from," said my guide, as I stood on the grassy hill after drinking copiously of the fountain of the Wye.

"We may," said I, "but before we do I must repeat some lines made by a man who visited these sources four hundred years ago." Then taking off my hat I lifted up my voice and sang:-

"From high Plynlimmon's shaggy side

Three streams in three directions glide ..."

"Nice pennillion, sir, I dare say," said my guide, "provided a person could understand them."

(Borrow 1862)

[on Cader Idris]

My old guide comes of a family of Welsh harpers ... he told me that he had once been up Cader Idris 4 times in one day for a £10 wager against a reading party of 4 or 5 Cambridge men who declared he could not do it. On the last day of September a pouring wet day he did it and won the wager easily. He could have gone up the 5th time.

Leaving the road we turned up a rough lane and crossing a little brook by a farm house were on the open mountain. The zig-zag path was steep in parts and a great wind blew over the mountain so that I had to sit down in a sheltered place and tie the band of my hat to my button-hole with the old guide's neckerchief, for, said the old man, 'Many hats have been lost on this ridge'. We aimed for a great stone on the top of the first ridge. After this the climbing was not so severe. The old man came up very slowly.

Soon after we passed the great stone we passed through a gateway the posts of which were large basaltic pillars. Here we saw a mountain standing apparently close by waiting upon Cader Idris. It was Plynlimmon. Here we passed round over the back of the mountain and began ascending the summit from the S. We came to a little round pool or rather hole full of water. The old man pulled a little tumbler out of his pocket rinsed it and gave me a glass of the clear bright water. It was delicious. Then he drank himself. He said the pool was the head water or spring of the Dysyni River. He had never known it dry in the driest summers. We saw from the spring the winding gleam of the Dysyni wandering down a desolate valley to join the Dyfi, its sister stream.

About this time the wind changed and flew suddenly round into the S. The head of Idris, which had been cowled in cloud, had cleared for a while, but now an impenetrable dark cloud settled down upon it and the mist came creeping down the mountain. The sky looked black and threatened rain. Now there lay before us vast tracts and belts of large stones lying so close together that no turf could be seen and no grass could grow between them ... Cader Idris is the stoniest, dreariest, most desolate mountain I was ever on. We came now to the edge of a vast gulf or chasm or bason almost entirely surrounded by black precipices rising from the waters of a small black tarn which lay at the bottom of the bason ... we stumbled and struggled on again over rough tracts and wildernesses of slate and basalt. The sun was shining on the hills below, but the mist crawled down and wrapped us as if in a shroud blotting out everything. The mists and clouds began to sweep by us in white thin ghostly sheets as if some great dread Presences and Powers were going past and we could only see the skirts of their white garments. The air grew damp and chill, the cloud broke on the mountain top and it began to rain. Now and then we could discern the black sharp peak which forms the summit looming large and dark through the cloud and rain and white wild driving mist, and it was hidden again. It is an awful place in a storm. I thought of Moses on Sinai.

The rain grew heavier. The old guide could not get on very fast and told me to go on alone to the top and shelter in the hut as I could not miss the path. So I went on up the last sharp peak looming black through the dark mist and cloud, by a winding path among the great rocks and wildernesses of loose stone. For a few minutes I was alone on the top of the mountain ... it is said that if anyone spends a night alone on the top of Cader ldris he will be found in the morning either dead or a mad-man or a poet gifted with the highest degree of inspiration...

We prepared to go down by the 'Foxes' Path'. And indeed it was a path fit only for foxes. After leading me a few steps he began to go over what seemed to me to be the edge of a precipice, depth unknown and hidden in the mist. The side of the mountain was frightfully steep here and required great care in going down. Suddenly the old man stopped at a beautiful little spring in the almost perpendicular bank, pulled out his tumbler and gave me a draught of the clear sparkling water, much colder than the water from the spring of Dysyni. About the spring the grass grew brilliant green and there was a long winding riband of bright green where the waters overflowing from the spring trickled down through the grass stems to feed the lake at which the foxes drink just below. Next we came to a broad belt of loose rocks lying close together which the guide cautioned me to beware of and not without reason saying they were as slippery as glass and that a sprained ankle was an awkward thing on the mountain. Down, down and out of the cloud into sunshine, all the hills below and the valleys were bathed in glorious sunshine - a wonderful and dazzling sight. Above and hanging overhead the vast black precipices towered and loomed through the clouds, and fast as we went down the mist followed faster and presently all the lovely sunny landscape was shrouded in a white winding sheet of rain. The path was all loose shale and stone and so steep that planting our alpenstocks from behind and leaning back upon them Alpine fashion we glissaded with a general land-slip, rush and rattle of shale and shingle down to the shore of the Foxes' Lake ... we passed another lake and after some rough scrambling walking over broken ground at the mountain foot we came back into the turnpike road ... As we entered Dolgelly the old man said, 'You're a splendid walker, Sir', a compliment which procured him a glass of brandy and water.

(Kilvert 13 June 1870)

The Lakes

Lakeland as ever was a sweet foretaste of heaven.

(Wainwright 1973)

There is an intrinsic charm about the Lake Country, and to me at least a music in the very names of Helvellyn and Skiddaw and Scawfell.

(Stephen 1901)

I do not indeed know any tract of country in which, within so narrow a compass, may be found an equal variety in the influence of light and shadow upon the sublime or beautiful features of landscape ... From a point between

Great Gavel [sic] and Scawfell, a shepherd would not require more than an hour to descend into any one of eight of the principal vales by which he would be surrounded ... yet, though clustered together, every valley has its distinct and separate character, in some instances, as if they had been formed in studied contrast to each other, and in others with the united pleasing differences and resemblances of a sisterly rivalship. This concentration of interest gives to the country a decided superiority over the most attractive districts of Scotland and Wales, especially for the pedestrian traveller.

(Wordsworth 1835)

Wordsworth was not, in the true sense, a walker. With him it was a mystical communion rather than an intimacy. He loved the country with a kind of austere and detached benevolence ... in his attitudes of thought there was probably little perceptible difference when he climbed Loughrigg after tea and when he took a whole day over the Langdale Pikes and Serjeant Man (if he ever did). He records expeditions, of course, but these were generally made with his wife and sister, which in the then state of feminine development would give little chance of walking. There is no evidence that he ever laid his body at full stretch to the conquest of mountain, hence they were to him merely mountains, full of general sublimities, but not individuals, each with its own idiosyncrasy, full of the variety and interest which are the staple food of friendship.

(Sidgwick 1912)

... those stronger emotions which a region of mountains is peculiarly fitted to excite. The base of those huge barriers may run for a long space in straight lines, and these parallel to each other, the opposite sides of a profound vale may ascend in exact counterparts, or in mutual reflection, like the billows of a troubled sea, and the impression be, from its very simplicity, more awful and sublime.

(Wordsworth 1835)

The ordinary walker, who gains that sudden jump and uplifting of his whole being as he approaches Esk Hause from the south-east, leaving behind the soft outlines and mere prettiness of the south, and on an instant lifts his head into a world of gods and giants.

(Sidgwick 1912)

> Up the Honister road we went
>
> At the full swing of deep content.
>
> We chatted at first of men and things
>
> And the Lakes and Lakeland happenings.
>
> But as we mounted, silence grew,
>
> And the hush of the mountains, far and wide,
>
> Over our trivial talk descended,
>
> While the great crags, austere and splendid,
>
> Clear-cut against the evening blue
>
> Closed in upon us from either side.
>
> It was a road for gods to tread.
>
> (Sidgwick 1918a)

[a quiet day on Skiddaw 1982]

The early morning is crystal clear - just the day for a stroll. The people of Keswick do it on Sunday afternoons.

On a good muddy bridle, past the monument to the two shepherds, it starts to drizzle. Into the open, raining and blowing. Steeply up in sleet as the valley is blotted out. Out on to the fell on a wide track with cairns. Snowing now, and very cold, with flakes blown horizontally - visibility twenty yards. Wind fierce, ground very slippery, and track obliterated. Turning into the wind it is hard to keep upright in the gusts. A brief shelter in a sheepfold before decision to retreat.

Turning downhill, crouching with small steps to avoid a wind-blown slide, with painful sleet blowing in the eyes. A stick is life-saving, and cairns are essential.

Out on to grass - need some calories, but buckle of sac is frozen. Shake out an impressive amount of snow, and stump back into sunny camp by Derwentwater.

(Tom Patterson)

Skiddaw, a giant in stature, but an affable and friendly giant.

(Wainwright 1961)

> We had been on the hills that day,
> And late in the afternoon we lay
> Prone and blown on a Haystack top,
> Watching the haze in a thin-drawn veil
> Gather and spread its arms and drop
> Over the crags of Ennerdale.
> The heights we had conquered lay behind,
> Ahead lay tea and the Honister road,
> And in the pure and vacuous mind
> A great, calm nothingness abode.
>
> (Sidgwick 1918a)

The Alps

... the very hub, the middle boss of all Europe, the rocky knot in which all her stone sinews are tied into one central bunch.

(Montague 1924)

The great men, it is true, have not always acknowledged their debt to the genius, whoever he may be, who presides over pedestrian exercise. Indeed, they have inclined to ignore the true source of their impulse. Even when they speak of the beauties of nature, they would give us to understand that they might have been disembodied spirits, taking aerial flights among mountain solitudes, and independent of the physical machinery of legs and stomachs.

When long ago the Alps cast their spell upon me, it was woven in a great degree by the eloquence of *Modern Painters*. I hoped to share Ruskin's ecstasies in a reverent worship of Mont Blanc and the Matterhorn. The influence of any cult, however, depends upon the character of the worshipper, and I fear that in this case the charm operated rather perversely. It stimulated a passion for climbing which absorbed my energies and distracted me from the prophet's loftier teaching. I might have followed him from the mountains to picture-galleries, and spent among the stones of Venice hours which I devoted to attacking hitherto unascended peaks and so losing my last chance of becoming an art critic. I became a fair judge of an Alpine guide, but I do not even know how to make a judicious allusion to Botticelli or Tintoretto. I can't say that I feel the smallest remorse. I had a good time, and at least escaped one temptation to talking nonsense. It follows, however, that my passion for the mountains had something earthly in its composition. It is associated with memories of eating and drinking.

I hold that Alpine walks are the poetry of the pursuit, I could try to justify the opinion by relating some of the emotions suggested by the great scenic effects ... But the thing has been done before, better than I could hope to do it.

(Stephen 1901)

You pig half the night in a hut, some way up, at the edge of the snow. At, say, two, you get up and go on. By Jove, it's still. You can hear every little whispering whistle of a wind that can't stir a thing, it's so small - only go leaping about in the dark, doing nothing. There's always a torrent a mile off in the valley, you go up and up and the noise of it thins away to a sort of hum of thought about some noise there used to be - you know the way, when you're going asleep, the thud in the street drones off into a dream about it. Next thing you look up with a start, the front man has stopped to put out the lantern, but ever so far off, over the Rhone, there's a grave russet light being held to the face of sleeping provinces ... Then our mountain fired his morning gun - first fall of rock for the day - crash into that staring, straining silence, like a stone gone bang into a window.

(Montague 1910)

Lake Neuchatel lay far below. With every step I took the distant Alps sank a fraction more until all but the most obtuse peaks pierced the horizon, and then they too began to subside. I would have held them back. I would have soared across that intervening space as you can soar in the boundless stuff of dreams, and climbed those heights then and there, recklessly, forgetful of all else except mastering the outworks, the first wall of the range I had thought about for so long, but that's not the way of walking. There's no escaping the persistent ordinariness, the dull lengths of prolonged exertion, and I walked on the quicker...

(Hillaby 1972)

[Belloc's first view of the Alps]

Just as I came to the end of the rise, after perhaps an hour, perhaps two, of that great curtain of forest which had held the mountain side, the trees fell away to brushwood, there was a gate, and then the path was lost upon a fine open sward which was the very top of the Jura ... It was evident that nothing higher remained, for though a new line of wood - firs and beeches - stood before me, yet nothing appeared above them, and I knew that they must be the fringe of the descent ... as I was looking for the entry of a path, there came to me one of those great revelations which betray to us suddenly the higher things and stand afterwards firm in our minds.

There, on the upper meadow, where so far I had felt nothing but the ordinary gladness of The Summit, I had a vision.

I saw between the branches of the trees in front of me a sight in the sky that made me stop breathing, just as great danger at sea, or great surprise in love, or a great deliverance will make a man stop breathing ... in between the branches of the trees was a great promise of unexpected lights beyond ... I found a place where the pine trees stopped, leaving a gap...

I looked through this framing hollow and praised God. For there below me, thousands of feet below me, was what seemed an illimitable plain, at the end of that world was an horizon, and the dim bluish sky that overhangs an horizon.

There was brume in it and thickness. One saw the sky beyond the edge of the world getting purer as the vault rose. But right up - a belt in that empyrean - ran peak and field and needle of intense ice, remote, remote from the world. Sky beneath them and sky above them, a steadfast legion, they glittered as though with the armour of the immovable armies of Heaven. Two days' march, three days' march away, they stood up like the walls of Eden.

I say it again, they stopped my breath. I had seen them...

Since I could now see such a wonder and it could work such things in my mind, therefore, some day I should be part of it. That is what I felt.

This it is also which leads some men to climb mountain-tops, but not me, for I am afraid of slipping down.

(Belloc 1902)

We came back last Thursday from our four weeks in the Alps, pretty fit and lean after some climbing that was as good for the body and the soul as ever. After 11 months here I want to go out and do something violent, the way dogs want to eat grass, and there is the deuce's own medicinal virtue in being done up and scorched and funked now and then and brought back to the primitive hardships and joys of physical self-dependence - or at least in playing at it. It's a rum thing that one simply loathes the mountains in some ways, for their beastly, dead-white blinding snow and drab, dirt-coloured rocks and their everlasting muck-heaps of moraines, and yet one is really in love - one aches with desire at 'em, though they're termagants.

(Montague 1912)

... the mighty dome of the Jungfrau, softly outlined against the sky and faintly silvered by the starlight. There was something subduing in the influence of that silent and solemn and awful presence, one seemed to meet the immutable, the indestructible, the eternal, face to face, and to feel the trivial and fleeting nature of his own existence the more sharply by the contrast. One had the sense of being under the brooding contemplation of a spirit, not an inert mass of rock and ice - a spirit which had looked down, through the slow drift of the ages, upon a million vanished races of men, and judged them, and would judge a million more - and still be there, watching, unchanged and unchangeable, after all life should be gone and the earth have become a vacant desolation.

While I was feeling these things, I was groping, without knowing it, towards an understanding of what the spell is which people find in the Alps, and in no other mountains - that strange, deep, nameless influence which, once felt, cannot be forgotten - once felt, leaves always behind it a restless longing to feel it again - a longing which is like homesickness, a grieving, haunting yearning, which will plead, implore, and persecute till it has its will. I met dozens of people, imaginative and unimaginative, cultivated and uncultivated, who had come from far countries and roamed through the Swiss Alps year after year - they could not explain why ... others said they could find perfect rest and peace nowhere else when they were troubled, all frets and worries and chafings sank to sleep in the presence of the benignant serenity of the Alps, the Great Spirit of the Mountains breathed his own peace upon their hurt minds and sore hearts, and healed them.

(Mark Twain 1880)

Italy

I looked down the vale, which was the gate of Tuscany. There - high, jagged, rapt into the sky - stood such a group of mountains as men dream of in good dreams, or see in the works of painters when old age permits them revelations. Their height was evident from the faint mist and grey of their hues, their outline was tumultuous, yet balanced: full of accident and poise. It was as though these high walls of Carrara, the western boundary of the valley, had been shaped expressly for man, in order to exalt him with unexpected and fantastic shapes, and to expand his dull life with a permanent surprise. For a long time I gazed at these great hills.

(Belloc 1902)

Central Italy is a paradise for the walker ... it is a land of hills and mountains, unenclosed, open in all directions to the wanderer at will, unlike some British mountain game-preserves.

And, even in the plain, the peasant, unlike some south-English farmers, never orders you off his ground, not even out of his olive grove or vineyard. The peasants are kind and generous to the wayfarer ... they will, without bargain or demur, gladly show you the way ... and Italian towns when you enter them, though it be at midnight, are still half awake, and everyone volunteers in the search to find you bed and board.

A siesta in the shade for three or four hours in the midday heat, to the tune of cicada and nightingale, is not the least pleasant part of all, and that means early starting and night walking, both very good things. The stars out there rule the sky more than in England, big and lustrous with the honour of having shone upon the ancients and been named by them.

(Trevelyan 1913)

After the Cambridge year ended, it became my custom in June to traverse some roadless Swiss pass into Italy. The long laborious pull up past the wooden chalets, through the deep snow and fir trees, and then on the other side the joyous run down through pastures of melting snow and opening crocus to forests of chestnut, and down through woodland paths to the ancient Alpine cities of Italy, was a game I loved to play. It was a real game with its chances, for sometimes the steep Swiss snow near the pass-top turned me back, and I had to try another valley-head.

In Italy my chief walking-grounds were the Tuscan and Umbrian hills ...

I kept to the high ground as much as I could, with the help of ordnance map and compass. I used to prolong my walks till late into the charmed Italian night, under those brilliant stars, known and named so long ago, at the right time of year I could walk after dark, mile after mile, to the continuous song of innumerable nightingales. There was also the prosaic inducement to walk on till one reached a sizable town ... where the inn was always awake at any midnight hour ... one was sure of excellent Italian food and local wine of the best, and other comforts welcome to the tired traveller.

(Trevelyan 1949)

The Appalachian Trail

The hardest part was coming to terms with the constant dispiriting discovery that there is always more hill. The thing about being on a hill, as opposed to standing back from it, is that you can almost never see exactly what's to come. Between the curtain of trees on every side, the ever-receding contour of rising slopes before you, and your own plodding weariness, you gradually lose track of how far you have come. Each time you haul yourself up to what you think must surely be the crest, you find that there is in fact more hill beyond, sloped at an angle that kept it from view before, and that beyond that slope there is another, and beyond that another and another, and beyond each of those more still, until it seems impossible that any hill could run on this long. Eventually you reach a height where you can see the tops of the topmost trees, with nothing but clear sky beyond, and your faltering spirit stirs - nearly there now! - but this is a pitiless deception. The elusive summit continually retreats by whatever distance you press forward, so that each time the canopy parts enough to give a view you are dismayed to see that the topmost trees are as remote, as unattainable, as before. Still you stagger on. What else can you do?

When, after ages and ages, you finally reach the telltale world of truly high ground, where the chilled air smells of pine sap and the vegetation is gnarled and tough and wind-bent, and push through to the mountain's open pinnacle, you are, alas, past caring.

You sprawl face down on a sloping pavement of gneiss, pressed to the rock by the weight of your pack, and lie there for some minutes, reflecting in a distant, out-of-body way that you have never before looked this closely at lichen, not in fact looked this closely and anything in the natural world since you were four years old and had your first magnifying glass. Finally, with a weary puff, you roll over, unhook yourself from your pack, struggle to your feet and realize - again in a remote, light-headed, curiously not-there way - that the view is sensational: a boundless vista of wooded mountains, unmarked by human hand, marching off in every direction. This really could be heaven. It's splendid, no question, but the thought you cannot escape is that you have to walk this view - and this is the barest fraction of what you will traverse before you have finished.

(Bryson 1997)

Himalayas

On the track up to Tjeng Boche a woman collapsed. The nearest escape would be to Lukla, a tiny ski-jump airstrip, from which she might be flown to Kathmandu, but this was two days away. The sirdar went back down the track to recruit a carrier, but it took time to find a sherpa willing to carry such a load uphill to Lukla - she was a big woman and semi-conscious. Finally a lad about one-third her weight agreed for Rs 500. A small plank was chopped and notched to hold the sling - as she was a woman, this was covered with a scrap of carpet found on the side of the track. She was loaded on to the sherpa's back with the sling round his forehead. He was pulled upright and pushed forward to get him started, with his T-stick to support the weight when resting. With the leader and sirdar on either side they reached Lukla in two days, and she was flown out safely

(Tom Patterson 1979)

I suppose I was already elated at approaching the Himalaya, the object of our pilgrimage, perhaps I was beginning to experience what - to borrow from the terminology of religious conversion - I can only describe as a change of heart.

Another experience invites comparison with the mountain-lover's in respect of the peculiar kind of felicity that it excites, I refer to mystical experience. There is, however, this difference, that the great mystics believe themselves to enter into direct communion with the absolute itself, while to the mountain-lover the sense of communion is not as a rule direct.

(Meade 1940)

... the delusion that somewhere, far off in the blue distance, lurks the Perfect Place, that the blue hills really are blue, that what one beholds is in its essence actually as beautiful as from above it seems - so long as that delusion lasts, Romance lingers.

In Kashmir - one of the culminating stations in my Pilgrimage of Romance, I had breasted a shoulder, some 10,000 feet high, and beheld a union of desert and mountains on a stupendous scale:

Mile and mile away the valley bent out of sight and great mountains closed it. Two tiny patches of irrigated green demonstrated the barrenness of all else. It was an overwhelming view, and I had come upon it suddenly round a corner. The world has seemed to me a more majestic place ever since. Moreover, this was no landscape of the moon, but one long associated with men. The track we had been following is of extreme antiquity. It must have been traversed by ancient invaders coming down from the north time after time, by Buddhist pilgrims, by followers of Islam with faces set towards Mecca, by merchants and travellers from earliest days. This they had also beheld. In wonder and reverence I drank in the vision.

(Conway 1933)

CHAPTER 5

HOW DID YOU GET THERE?

There is no orthodoxy in Walking. It is a land of many paths and no-paths, where everyone goes his own way and is right.

(Trevelyan 1913)

Just watch a man walking, if he is a proper man, and see the business of it: how he expresses his pride, or his determination, or his tenacity, or his curiosity, or perhaps his very purpose in his stride! Well, all that business of walking that you are looking at is a piece of extraordinarily skilful trick-acting, such that were the animal not known to do it you would swear he could never be trained to it by any process, however lengthy, or however minute, or however strict.

Not only do you manage to do it, but you can do it in a thousand ways, as a really clever acrobat will astonish his audience not only by walking on a tight-rope but by eating his dinner on it. You can walk quickly or slowly, or look over your shoulder as you walk, or shoot fairly accurately as you walk, you can saunter, you can force your pace, you can turn which way you will. You certainly did not teach yourself to accomplish this marvel, nor did your nurse.

(Belloc 1911)

Your feet occupy the centre of your little world, and you watch them stepping out left, right, left, right, over the wet grass, and you wonder how they keep on doing it without making a mistake. Left, right, left, right, they go interminably. What would happen if they went left, right, left, left, right? The problem fascinates. You try it, you exert all your willpower to make them blunder, but they will not. You conclude that their actions are not controlled by your brain, after all.

(Wainwright 1986)

[There are] four great classes of walker - the six-miler, the twelve-miler, the eighteen-miler, and the twenty-four miler - which are separated by more than a numerical distinction.

Class A, the twenty-four milers, average about 4½ miles an hour on a good road, and stride 40 inches or over: they tend to be mugwumps [independent], mistrusters of rhetoric, lovers of the classic in art and music and literature, of the distilled and clarified products of human imagination or insight. Class B, the eighteen milers, average 4 miles an hour, and stride 36 inches: they are generally those who might have been in Class A but for a lack of real comprehensive capacity and for a love of talking and disputation, they read Meredith, but talk about his philosophy, and have no proper grasp of Dickens. Class C, average 3½ miles an hour and call it 'about 4', and stride 30 inches: they often have Class A capacities, but are physically disabled: they insist on large meals and a good deal of drink, and talk much of 'scorching'. Class D, average 2½ miles an hour, and stride 25 inches: they have no illusions about either, and are mainly occupied in catching a train home at the earliest opportunity.

(Sidgwick 1912)

There are good walkers and bad walkers, and the difference between them has nothing to do with performance in mileage or speed. The difference lies in the way they put their feet down. A good walker is a *tidy* walker. He moves quietly, places his feet where his eyes tell him to, on beaten tracks treads firmly, avoids loose stones on steep ground, disturbs nothing. He is, by habit, an improver of paths.

A bad walker is a *clumsy* walker. He moves noisily, disturbs the surface and even the foundations of paths by kicking up loose stones, tramples the verges until they disintegrate into debris. He is, by habit, a maker of bad tracks and a spoiler of good ones. A good walker's special joy is zigzags, which he follows faithfully. A bad walker's special joy is in shortcutting and destroying zigzags.

(Wainwright 1966)

The claims of walking to a place among the staple forms of athletics seem dubious. Every one would agree that it takes place in the open air, not many that it is hard exercise, fewer still that it involves physical expertness ... the walker's motions are things, apparently, which anyone can do.

None the less, walking at its best comes very near the greater athletics. A full day's walk at a good pace is not a thing to be despised ... walking is no activity for the grossly untrained or incapable ... there is the special demon of inertia always waiting for you at the eighth mile, and again about the eighteenth, ready to seize on the slightest weakness, a demon only to be exorcised by a genuine effort. If you can conquer him, you may at least claim a leaf from the athlete's crown. In the matter of physical expertness ... a proper stride is not a mere gift from the gods, it can be cultivated, increased in ease and length, made a more useful servant. There is no little difference at the end of the day between the walker who can move his feet lithely and delicately, making a rhythmic bar of each stride, and the walker who hoists them up anyhow and lets them fall with a bang, like instruments of percussion. The adjustment of gait to slopes and to varying types of ground is also a matter of some expertness.

Athletes, in the utmost rigour of their training, use walking as one of the most effective means ... there must surely be something in walking akin to, if not identical with, the highest capacities of the body, when a man is reaching his physical maximum, he does not grouse-shoot or beagle or dance or play billiards, but he does walk.

(Sidgwick 1912)

The English pedestrian has the advantage of us [Americans] in the matter of climate, for notwithstanding the traditional gloom and moroseness of English skies, they have none of those relaxing, sinking, enervating days, of which we have so many here - days which withdraw all support from the back and loins, and render walking of all things burdensome.

Then their land is threaded with paths which invite the walker.

Then the English claim that they are a more hearty and robust people than we are. It is certain they are a plainer people, have plainer tastes, dress plainer, build plainer, speak plainer, keep closer to facts, wear broader shoes and coarser clothes, place a lower estimate on themselves, etc. - all of which traits favour pedestrian habits.

(Burroughs 1875)

There is a world of difference between swinging along without a pack and trudging along carrying thirty or forty pounds. The unencumbered walker is a digitigrade, a toe-user. He leans forward in such a way that he glides along, scarcely seeming to touch the ground. Energy for the initial push off is provided by the ball of the foot and, almost immediately afterwards, by the big toe. Once you get going the power is supplemented by gravity controlled by the rhythmical movements of the legs. The movement is a marvellous one. Step by step, the body teeters on the edge of catastrophe...

By contrast, the gait of a burdened man is inclined to be flat-footed or plantigrade. Until you get accustomed to the change in posture you lumber along like a caveman. But with practice the pack can be carried high and balanced in such a way that after a week or two of weight-lifting you feel unbalanced without it.

(Hillaby 1972)

[in Hungary with a fiddle on his back]

It was a grilling day and my legs were not yet used to tramping. I walked heavily on my heels without any fixed rhythm and so by the time I had covered eight miles I was footsore and weary. I then remembered how a tramp had once told me that it was much easier to go on for hours and hours if one jogged forward on the point part of the feet in a shuffling gait, always keeping to the same rhythm. "Once you fall into the jog-trot," said he, "you move mechanically and feel no fatigue."

(Starkie 1933)

My guide walked with a calm and deliberate gait, yet I had considerable difficulty in keeping up with him. There was, however, nothing surprising in this, he was a shepherd walking on his own hill, and having first-rate wind, and knowing every inch of the ground, made great way without seeming to be in the slightest hurry: I would not advise a road-walker, even if he be a first-rate one, to attempt to compete with a shepherd on his own, or indeed any hill, should he do so, the conceit would soon be taken out of him.

(Borrow 1862)

In a valley of the Apennines, a little before it was day, I went down by the side of a torrent wondering where I should find repose, for it was now some hours since I had given up all hope of discovering a place for proper human rest and for the passing of the night.

As I still trudged, half expectant and half careless, a man came up behind me, walking quickly as do mountain men: for throughout the world (I cannot tell why) I have noticed that the men of the mountains walk quickly and in a sprightly manner, arching the foot, and with a light and general gait as though the hills were waves and as though they were in thought springing upon the crests of them. This is true of all mountaineers. They are but few.

(Belloc 1908)

... getting back on to the London road, I forgot everything but the way ahead. I walked steadily, effortlessly, hour after hour, in a kind of swinging, weightless dream. I was at that age which feels neither strain nor friction, when the body burns magic fuels, so that it seems to glide in warm air, about a foot off the ground, smoothly obeying its intuitions. Even exhaustion, when it came, had a voluptuous quality, and sleep was caressive and deep, like oil. It was the peak of the body's total extravagance, before the accounts start coming in.

(Laurie Lee 1969)

It was nearing half-past six: my train was 7.22: my station four miles away. I was in exactly the mood, and my legs had reached the precise stage of stiffness, in which walking is best and easiest, not with the supple and careless ease of the morning, which tempts one to excess, but with the matured and disciplined ease which comes of a long day, the consummation of labours endured and experience gained. The ancient pack-horse track lay straight ahead ... was it not worth everything to have achieved this moment?

(Sidgwick 1918b)

> I love a public road: few sights there are
> That please me more, such object hath had power
> O'er my imagination since the dawn
> Of childhood, when its disappearing line,
> Seen daily afar off, on one bare steep
> Beyond the limits which my feet had trod
> Was like a guide into eternity,
> At least to things unknown and without bound.
>
> (Wordsworth, *Prelude Book XII*)

By road

Much has been written of travel, far less of the road. Writers have treated the road as a passive means to an end, and honoured it most when it has been an obstacle, they leave the impression that a road is a connection between two points which only exists when the traveller is upon it.

The earliest roads wandered like rivers through the land, having, like rivers, one necessity, to keep in motion. We still say that a road "goes" to London, as we "go" ourselves. We point out a white snake on a green hillside, and tell a man: "That is going to Chichester."

It is a silent companion always ready for us, whether it is night or day, wet or fine, whether we are calm or desperate, well or sick. It is always going, it has never gone right away, and no man is too late.

(Edward Thomas 1913)

The face of any old road is as visibly filled with expression and lined with experience as any old man's. Take the mere point of straightness and crookedness. A road, like a piece of string, goes straight when the strongest pull is from end to end, it goes crooked when the strongest pulls are to this side and that.

(Montague 1924)

There's a narrow road through the [Duddon] valley, which twists and turns and goes round little hummocks...Lakeland roads, the minor ones of course, are a pleasure to walk, as long as you don't choose to walk them on Easter Sunday. They follow the contours yet they're above the contours. You can look up and down and all around without having to bother to watch your feet the way you do on the fells. Fell walkers scorn roads of any sort - which is silly. It's traffic which is terrible, not tarmac.

(Hunter Davies 2000)

The plain road was made beautiful by the many thoughts it gave. I came every morning to stay by the star-lit bank

A friend said, "Why do you go the same road every day? Why not have a change and walk somewhere else sometimes? Why keep on up and down the same place?" I could not answer, till then it had not occurred to me that I did always go one way, as for the reason of it I could not tell, I continued in my old mind while the summers went away.

Not till years afterwards was I able to see why I went the same round and did not care for change. I do not want change: I want the same old and loved things ... and I want them in the same place ... I would follow the plain old road to-day if I could. Let change be far from me, that irresistible change must come is bitter indeed.

(Jefferies 1909)

The road as an emblem of life ... with its milestones for years, its direction posts to show you the way, its inns for feasting, its churches for prayer, its cross-roads for destiny, its happy corners of love and meeting, its sad ones of bereavement and farewell, its backward vista of memory, its forward one of hope.

(Graham 1927)

The Road ... we take it so much for granted that its original meaning escapes us. Men, indeed, whose pleasure it is perpetually to explore even their own country on foot, and to whom its every phase of climate is delightful, receive, somewhat tardily, the spirit of The Road. They feel a meaning in it, it grows to suggest the towns upon it, it explains its own vagaries, and it gives a unity to all that has arisen along its way. But for the mass The Road is silent, it is the humblest and the most subtle, but the greatest and the most original of the spells which we inherit from the earliest pioneers of our race. It was the most imperative and the first of our necessities. It is older than building and than wells, before we were quite men we knew it, for the animals still have it today, they seek their food and their drinking places, and, as I believe, their assemblies, by known tracks which they have made.

(Belloc 1924)

To recover a Roman road, to establish its exact alignment, even in detail, is not one of those half-futile historic tasks, whose achievement ends in itself. The research has indeed its "sporting" side. It presents all the fascination that attaches to any form of hunting, with that element added which comes from the tracking of a trail in the open air, and if the establishment of a Roman road had no other excuse but this element of interest, the excuse would be ample for the work involved.

(Belloc 1913)

Watling Street, the most superb of all the Roman roads ... behind me and before me it held its stern and inflexible straight line. We Londoners call it the Edgware Road, and know it as a shopping centre, full of picture palaces. None the less, legions once marched along it.

(Sidgwick 1918b)

[near Lake Como]

The path itself was a miracle, so easy to follow and so certain. I'd forgotten how paths had their own cognition, their way of introducing the past. They carried in their sunken beds the footfalls of long-gone travellers and in their air the smell of bridles and the ring of iron and bronze. Romans had come here.

(Crane 1997)

What, under modern conditions, is the country walker to do? He cannot, it is clear, walk on the roads.

Hence all that literature of walking and walking tours in which the English language is so rich, of which the essays of Hazlitt and Stevenson and Richard Jefferies are luminous examples, is hopelessly out of date. For it is mainly a literature of road walking.

(Joad 1932)

Yet the hard road plays a part in every good walk, generally at the beginning and at the end. Nor must we forget the "soft" road, mediating as it were between his hard artificial brother and wild surrounding nature. The broad green lanes of the low country, relics of mediaeval wayfaring, the green unfenced moorland road, the derelict road already half gone back to pasture, the common farm track - these and all their kind are a blessing to the walker ... for they unite the speed and smooth surface of the harder road with much at least of the softness to the foot, the romance and the beauty of cross-country routes.

(Trevelyan 1913)

There is much to be said for a good spell of road taken at a steady pace, especially in company, there is no need to worry about ground and direction, and the mind is free and can sink into contemplation.

(Sidgwick 1918b)

The road-walkers are the Puritans of the religion. A strain of fine ascetic rigour is in these men. Stevenson is *par excellence* their bard. They have grasped one part of the truth. The road is invaluable for pace and swing, and the ideal walk permits or even requires a smooth surface for some considerable part of the way.

Bowen[1] kept at home what he used to call his "road-map", an index outline of the ordnance survey of our island, ten miles to the inch, on which he marked his walks in red ink. It was the chief part of his life to cover every part of the map with those red spider-webs. He generally kept to the roads from preference for the free and steady sway of leg over level surface which attracts Stevenson and all devotees of the road.

(Trevelyan 1913)

---

[1] Edward Bowen, house-master at Harrow in 1892, was the first of the very few who have walked the eighty miles from Cambridge to Oxford in the twenty-four hours (Trevelyan 1949)

On other terms it is hard to cover a respectable distance, and the change of tactile values underfoot is agreeable.

But more than that I will not concede: twenty-five or thirty miles of moor and mountain, of wood and field-path, is better in every way than five-and-thirty, or even forty, hammered out on the road.

(Trevelyan 1913)

Railway tracks

I am fond of walking along railway tracks. They are frequently little canyons running through deep cuttings, the banks of which are ablaze with flowers. (Flowers seem to like railway cuttings, somebody once gave me a good botanical reason for this, but I forget what it was. Presence of smoke, perhaps, or absence of motorists!) Single line tracks, moreover, often traverse deserted and forgotten country - in this respect, by the way, they are like canals - and the sleepers are placed at just the right distance to accommodate the stride.

(Joad 1946)

The inconveniently spaced railway sleepers gave me the gait of a man who couldn't remember which leg had been amputated.

(Crane 1997)

Old railways don't fade away - they turn into unique nature reserves. While chemicals have killed almost all natural life on either side of the railways, the embankments have always had their own plant and animal life. In the last decade, much of this life has been left completely undisturbed, allowed to grow wild, unmolested, unseen.

As on all railway lines, there is the tantalising switchback feeling of going up and down, one moment looking out across fields as the track appears to rise up, the next deep in a gorge, with embankments towering either side. In reality, you hardly ever rise or fall very much.

No matter where you live in Britain, there is an old disused railway line not very far away, overgrown perhaps, probably overlooked, certainly undervalued. They are unique botanical corridors, treasure trails full of local historical, social, industrial and architectural interest, all of them just waiting to be explored.

(Hunter Davies 1982)

Walking as a sport

The one thing which never, nowhere, and under no conditions is, was, or could be a sport, is walking.

An exception might be made for walking of the racing type. The walking race is indeed a wonderful thing, a standing testimony to the exuberance of human invention. Naturally, if a man wants to go fast, he runs, if he wants to go at a steady pace for a long distance, he walks. Only in the higher stages of civilisation, when his mind really gets to work, does he invent a mode of progression which combines all the possible disadvantages, being more exhausting than a walk, slower than a run, physically uncomfortable ... no one who has seen the gait of a walking racer can ever forget it.

We may, if we please, fondly imagine that walking involves a fair struggle with time and space, with rocks and hills, but this is mere playing with words. The true sporting relation can only exist between man and man, never between man and things ... in walking you do not wait until weather and ground are at their worst in order to give them a chance of defeating you, you take the most favourable opportunities, you steal advantages, you employ all the cunning of the organism to overcome the inorganic. A walker needs many qualities for the pursuit of his craft - endurance, equability, resource, a good conscience, both moral and physical, but the one thing which, as walker, he never needs is the sporting instinct.

(Sidgwick 1912)

Test walking

Early in life, no doubt, a man will test himself at pace Walking, and then of course the road must be kept. Every aspiring Cantab and Oxonian ought to walk to the Marble Arch at a pace that will do credit to the college whence he starts at break of day: the wisdom of our ancestors, surely not by an accident, fixed those two seats of learning each at the same distance from London, and at exactly the right distance for a test walk ... start at five from Cambridge, and have a second breakfast ordered beforehand at Royston to be ready at eight.

And there is a harder test than that: if a man can walk the eighty miles from St Mary Oxon to St Mary Cantab in the twenty-four hours, he wins his place with Bowen (p. 102 f.n.) and a very few more.

(Trevelyan 1913)

Record-breaking

Record-breaking is, of course, a possible form of walking, and most of us have indulged in it at one time or another, it is interesting and sometimes even salutary, to abandon all higher thoughts, and go for a record frankly and whole-heartedly. But to the true walker this is only an occasional indulgence. Record-breaking is ultimately a degrading and (literally) a brutalising pastime. It is the mere pitting of the brute animal powers against the brute inanimate conditions of time and space. If we are to be men and not animals, walking must be something more than a mere swing of the legs, and the country something more than a colourless aliquantum of miles. Record-breaking, if it becomes a habit, will be as a blight in the fair garden of walking, as a sarrusophone in the pedestrian symphony.

(Sidgwick 1912)

Long distance

It is little to a man's profit to go far afield if his chief pleasure be in wild life, his main object to get nearer to the creatures, to grow day by day more intimate with them, and to see each day some new thing. Yet the distance has the same fascination for him as for another - the call is as sweet and persistent in his ears. If he is on a green level country with blue hills on the horizon, then, especially in the early morning, is the call sweetest, most irresistible.

Come away - come away, this blue world has better things than any in that green, too familiar place.

(Hudson 1909)

William Hutton, a business-man in Birmingham, in July 1801 at the age of seventy-eight, walked from Birmingham to Carlisle. He then walked the full length of the Roman Wall and back, "having crossed the kingdom twice, under a burning sun and without a drop of rain, in seven days and six hours". After resting for a few days, he walked back to Birmingham. He had been away thirty-five days, spent forty guineas, and covered 601 miles in one pair of shoes.

"So long and solitary a journey on foot was perhaps never wantonly performed by a man of seventy-eight. It has excited the curiosity of the town and causes me frequently to be stopped in the street to ascertain the fact."

(Murray 1939)

[De Quincey in 1802 aged 17]

No sort of disgrace attached in Wales, as too generally upon the great roads of England, to the pedestrian style of travelling. Indeed, the majority of those I met as fellow-tourists in the quiet little cottage-parlours of the Welsh posting-houses were pedestrian travellers ... everywhere at intermitting distances of twelve to sixteen miles, I found the most comfortable inns. And it has often struck me that a world-wearied man could not do better than revolve amongst these modest inns in the five northern Welsh counties.

Sleeping, for instance, and breakfasting at Carnarvon, then, by an easy nine-mile walk, going forwards to dinner at Bangor, thence to Aber - nine miles, or to Llanberris, and so on for ever, accomplishing seventy to ninety or one hundred miles in a week. This, upon actual experiment, and for week after week, I found the most delightful of lives ... if the weather were but tolerable, through endless successions of changing beauty, and towards evening a courteous welcome in a pretty rustic home - quite peculiar to Wales was in those days (I hope in these) the Welsh harp, in attendance at every inn.

Life on this model was but too delightful, and to myself especially, that am never thoroughly in health unless when having pedestrian exercise to the extent of fifteen miles at the most, and eight to ten miles at the least.

(De Quincey 1821)

[Canon A. N. Cooper walked from Yorkshire to Rome in 40 days in 1887]

A paragraph he chanced upon in Ruskin set him off. The author of *Modern Painters* believed that no one would again cross Europe on foot. The proper feel of Europe, which comes to a man through his toes, would be lost for ever. Cooper was determined to confute Ruskin.

(Murray 1939)

It is only at the end of a long and solitary day's walk that I have had strange, casual moments of mere sight and feeling more vivid and less forgotten than the human events of life, moments like those that Wordsworth has described as his common companions in boyhood ... these come to me only after five-and-twenty miles.

(Trevelyan 1913)

>And I have felt
>
>A presence that disturbs me with the joy
>
>Of elevated thoughts, a sense sublime
>
>Of something far more deeply interfused,
>
>Whose dwelling is the light of setting suns,
>
>And the round ocean and the living air,
>
>And the blue sky, and in the mind of man:
>
>A motion and a spirit, that impels
>
>All thinking things, all objects of all thought,
>
>And rolls through all things.
>
>(Wordsworth 1798)

Wordsworth's vision and power were closely connected with his long daily walks. De Quincey tells us: "I calculate that Wordsworth must have traversed a distance of 175,000 of 180,000 English miles, a mode of exertion which to him stood in the stead of alcohol and all stimulants whatsoever, to which indeed he was indebted for a life of unclouded happiness, and we for much of what is most excellent in his writings."

(Trevelyan 1913)

He who is indeed of the brotherhood does not voyage in quest of the picturesque, but of certain jolly humours - of the hope and spirit with which the march begins at morning, and the peace and spiritual repletion of the evening's rest. He cannot tell whether he puts his knapsack on, or takes it off, with more delight. The excitement of the departure puts him in key for that of the arrival. Whatever he does is not only a reward in itself, but will be further rewarded in the sequel, and so pleasure leads on to pleasure in an endless chain. It is this that so few can understand: they will either be always lounging or always at five miles an hour, they do not play off the one against the other, prepare all day for the evening, and all evening for the next day. And, above all, it is here that your overwalker fails of comprehension ... he will not believe that to walk this unconscionable distance is merely to stupefy and brutalise himself, and come to his inn, at night, with a sort of frost on his five wits, and a starless night of darkness in his spirit.

(Stevenson 1889)

I am beginning to have second thoughts about "official" long-distance footpaths. I am now not at all sure that they are wholly to be commended ... the wide publicity given to them bring disadvantages. The official blessing and opening of a long-distance path is headline news. The word goes forth and the world pulls on his boots.

The first of them, the Pennine Way, has already been so much used that it is fast losing its appeal as a wilderness walk and becoming a too-popular parade ... in time you won't need a map: just follow the trail of empty cans and orange peel.

(Wainwright 1973)

More people are retiring early and they are living longer. They seek an activity which is economically and medically prudent. Hill-walking fits the bill.

At some point control is deemed necessary and Park Wardens are employed to direct the traffic ... If this type of control goes against the grain, yet we accept that some control is necessary, what form is it to take? I would not go so far as the elitist suggestion that the Nature Conservancy should build moats around all worth-while mountains and fill them waist-deep with slurry, the only 'clean' point of access to be thirty-foot rockfaces at mild severe standard or harder.

(Wilson 1998)

Cross-country

The secret beauties of nature are unveiled only to the cross-country walker: the sudden glory of a woodland glade, the open back-door of the old farmhouse sequestered deep in rural solitude, the cow routed up from meditation behind the stone wall as we scale it suddenly, the deep, slow, south-country stream that we must jump, or wander along to find the bridge, the northern torrent of molten peat-hag that we must ford up to the waist, to scramble, glowing warm-cold, up the farther foxglove bank, the autumnal dew on the bracken and the blue straight smoke of the cottage in the still glen at dawn, the rush down the mountain-side, hair flying, stones and grouse rising at our feet, and at the bottom the plunge in the pool below the waterfall, in a place so fair that kings should come from far to bathe therein - yet is it left, year in year out, unvisited save by us and "troops of stars". These, and a thousand other blessed chances of the day, are the heart of Walking, and these are not of the road.

(Trevelyan 1913)

Personally I have always preferred cross-country walking to any other kind, and should still to a very large extent go across country, even if the roads were tolerable and it were not forbidden. You get more varied walking that way than any other, to go across a field and over a hedge, through a copse, and then over another hedge into an orchard, and so through a gate into a farmyard with barking dogs, and to be followed by a quarter of a mile down a lane and then up a bank and over another hedge and so into the fields again is for me the ideal type of normal walking.

(Joad 1932)

You are going to be very ill-mannered and stray on to other people's property. Granted that fundamental impertinence you must be as nice as possible about it, graciously lift your hat to the proprietor when you see him. You should be as careful to do as little damage as possible, mend the hedge you have broken, put back the hurdle, avert your face if a lady is swimming in her private pool.

It is enough to do the walk roughly. You cannot follow a ruled straight line across sown fields and flower beds and through the lord of the manor's kitchen ... the main idea is to see just what the land of a given country is like and to enjoy it. You have the added thrill of not knowing whom you will meet and on what terms.

(Graham 1927)

... the peculiar virtue of walking to a far place, and especially of walking there in a straight line, that one gets these visions of the world from hilltops ... It is only by following the straight line onwards that any one can pass from ridge to ridge and have this full picture of the way he has been.

(Belloc 1902)

Tortuosities are never objectless, and often lead to exceptionally fascinating pieces of scenery, yet there is lacking that grandeur of conception about the walk as a whole, that sense of a sustained purpose, which attaches to a straight-line walk of twenty miles or more. There is a certain sublimity, such as the Roman road-makers must have felt, in holding a general direction across country regardless of the rise and fall of the ground, most of all when the direction is southward, and the sun swings slowly round from the left cheek to the nose and on to the right cheek and the right ear. So man goes straight to his goal while the constellations swing round him.

(Sidgwick 1912)

Downhill

[Coleridge coming straight down Scafell Pike]

There is one sort of Gambling, to which I am addicted, and that not of the least inimical kind for a Man who has Children and a Concern. It is this. When I find it convenient to descend from a Mountain, I am too confident and too indolent to look around about and wind about 'till I find a track or other symptom of safety, but I wander on, where it is first possible to descend, there I go - relying upon fortune for how far down this possibility will continue. So it was yesterday afternoon.

(Kenny 1991)

The art of scree-running lies in travelling as fast as, or faster than, the little avalanche of stones upon which the climber is riding. If he should travel less quickly than the avalanche, the ground slips away from under his feet.

(Borthwick 1939)

[Wainright on coming downhill]

The only serious bit of advice he will give, and even then he says it is common-sense, is to try to keep the feet pointing slightly upwards when coming downhill, taking advantage of any tufts or stones to act as a brake. If all else fails, don't be afraid to slide down. 'A walker's best asset can be a tough, rubbery bottom. The posterior is a valuable agent of friction, a sheet anchor with superb resistance to the pull of gravity.'

(Hunter Davies 2000)

Running on a walk

There is the very subtle art, when you are coming down a steepening hill, of knowing the moment at which to abandon care, swing out and run.

It is quite unlike ordinary running, it generally takes place down a violent slope and could not possibly be managed in spiked shoes and bare legs. Running down a hard grass hill is good, on the flat of the foot, with short strides, each step sending a jerk from the extreme toe to the topmost hair, then, as the slope flattens near the bottom, you swing out, stride enormously and fly. Thus do, descending from Scarf Gap to Buttermere, and turn to the left at the foot beyond the stream, to the pool with the grassy promontory which washes you clean of mortal ills.

Scree-running is good, when you have clambered gingerly down the crags, and find them issuing below in fine slopes of shale, here forget your toes, trust only to your heels, and look out for rocks.

But best of all is the grassy head of a valley, soft with moss and hidden bog, here you must rush at full stride, watching your leader (if there is one) for bog-holes, if not, trusting in Providence. If your foot fall on good ground, it is well, if there be a sudden yielding beneath it, leap but more wildly off the other, and it will rise from the bog with a sound like a giant's kiss, and a tingle of cold water within your boot. Thus come wise men from Esk Hause to Borrodale by Grain Gill, forsaking the path of the foolish by Styhead Pass, and at the bottom there is a pool for them only less worthy than that of Buttermere, and thereafter they move down Borrodale in the dusk among silent sheep-folds, ennobled and perfected men, the long memories of the day rounded with the rapture of their run.

(Sidgwick 1912)

[guided by John Jones in the hills above Llangollen]

We passed over the summit, and began to descend by a tolerably good, though steep road. But for the darkness of evening and a drizzling mist, which, for some time past, had been coming on, we should have enjoyed a glorious prospect down the valley, or perhaps I should say that I should have enjoyed a glorious prospect, for John Jones, like a true mountaineer, cared not a brass farthing for prospects. The mist soon wetted us to the skin notwithstanding that we put up our umbrellas. It was a regular Welsh mist ... As we descended, the path became more steep. Here, finding walking very difficult, I determined to run. So shouting to John Jones, I set off running down the pass. My companion followed close behind, and luckily meeting no mischance, we presently found ourselves on level ground.

(Borrow 1862)

Scrambling

If the walker seeks variety of bodily motion, other than the run down hill, let him scramble. Scrambling is an integral part of Walking, when the high ground is kept all day in a mountain region. To know and love the texture of rocks we should cling to them, and when mountain-ash or holly, or even the gnarled heather root, has helped us at a pinch, we are thenceforth on terms of affection with all their kind. No one knows how sun and water can make a steep bank of moss smell like ambrosia till he has dug foot, fingers and face into it in earnest. And you must learn to haul yourself up a rock before you can visit those fern-clad inmost secret places where the Spirit of the Gully dwells.

(Trevelyan 1913)

Climbing

But the nineteenth century atmosphere was unfavourable for its beginnings. Prosperous security saw in it only a dangerous eccentricity, Queen Victoria even suggested its being forbidden, and our national mistrust of aesthetic or romantic sentiment made suspect, also, a novel impulse that could be traced back to the influence of poets and artists.

(Young 1936)

Of climbing I can write nothing, it is an amusement or a gamble that I have had no opportunity of enjoying.

(Belloc 1911)

... the need for the serious hill walker to ascend or, more particularly, descend relatively steep but technically easy rock. By serious hill walker, I mean someone who intends to climb Scottish mountains in the summer months ... It would therefore seem sensible that the serious hill walker should feel comfortable enough to solo the lowest technical rock climbing grades, as without this accomplishment he could get himself into as much trouble as walking in winter without ice axe and crampons.

(Wilson 2002)

It may be argued that scrambling and its elder brother climbing are the essence of Walking made perfect. I am not a climber and cannot judge. But I acknowledge in the climber the one person who, upon the whole, has not good reason to envy the walker. On the other hand, those stalwart Britons who, for their country's good, shut themselves up in one flat field all day and play there, surrounded by ropes and a crowd, may keep themselves well and happy, but they are divorced from nature.

(Trevelyan 1913)

I'd leave the real rock climbs for the professionals. They can spend all day on one slab, gripping it, searching its hidden crevices, its secret orifices, waiting and caressing, coupling and poking, inserting and pulling, their ropes stiff and taut, working themselves slowly into position as they jerk themselves forward in fits, in starts, till the moment of supreme climax when they reach their peak and lie exhausted on the top, all passion spent, their lifelines hanging limp and lifeless. Not my idea of fun, or even sublimation. Give me a grassy path along the fellside any old day.

(Hunter Davies 2000)

Short cuts

The Spaniards have a proverb: "No hay atajo sin trabajo," there is no short cut without a deal of labour. This proverb is very true, as I know by my own experience, for I never took a short cut in my life, and I have taken many in my wanderings, without falling down, getting into a slough, or losing my way.

(Borrow 1862)

[Leith Hill]

To me the panorama suggests a whole network of paths, which have been the scene of personally conducted expeditions, in which I displayed the skill on which I most pride myself - skill, I mean, in devising judicious geographical combinations, and especially of contriving admirable short cuts. The persistence of some companions in asserting that my short cuts might be the longest way round shows that the best of men are not free from jealousy.

(Stephen 1901)

[in the Pyrenees]

... where you think you see a short cut, and the map gives you no track, there the short cut is to be avoided ... the path sometimes takes such apparently needless turns that you are for escaping it by an easier cut.

You will never succeed. You may indeed succeed in a bit of exceptionally hard climbing, you may not lose your life, but you will most certainly wish that you had never attempted the unmarked crossing of the ridge you have attacked.... these mountains are full of vengeance, and hate to be disturbed.

(Belloc 1909)

Beelining

It is never possible to follow a dead-straight beeline over a long distance without trespassing: climbing fences, wading rivers, perhaps swimming sheets of water, and walking through houses and gardens. In fact, no straight line on a map will give a dead-straight beeline because it is now generally accepted in the best circles that the earth is round, not flat, and a straight line on a map must therefore be incorrect to the extent of the curvature between the two points, however slight.

(Wainwright 1973)

I nipped over a fence quietly, and put my foot down among an enormous flock of free-ranging but, at that moment, quietly dozing white Leghorns. Instant consternation. Off they went, like unguided missiles ... the skull cinema promptly snapped on a bit of comedy relief ... when the last British forces in France were trying to get out ... we crouched under the eaves of a Normandy farmhouse ... the men speculated on the sex and edibility of the poultry and started to offer odds on the outcome of a chase between a rooster and a fat hen. When the rooster was just about to mount the cornered bird, it saw a worm. The foolish animal stopped and ate it, enabling the hen to escape. 'By gum!' said a Yorkshire bombardier, 'Ah've niver bin as 'ungry as that.'

(Hillaby 1968)

[beaten back on the Gries Pass]

I was delighted to find it still raining. A dense mist above the rain gave me still greater pleasure. I had started at my leisure late in the day, and I did the thing stolidly, and my heart was like a dully-heated mass of coal or iron because I was acknowledging defeat. You who have never taken a straight line and held it, nor seen strange men and remote places, you do not know what it is to have to go round by the common way.

(Belloc 1902)

In the country a real cross-section and haphazard and adventurous tramp is one which can be known as "Trespassers' Walk." You take with you a little compass, decide to go west or east, as fancy favours, and then keep resolutely to the guidance of the magnetic needle. It takes you the most extraordinary way, and shows what an enormous amount of the face of the earth is kept away from the feet of ordinary humanity by the fact of "private property." On the other side of the hedge that skirts the public way is an entirely different atmosphere and company.

You are in a turnip field, which you skirt. In your next field you see a fearsome animal all by himself, grazing at leisure, and it depends on your courage whether you will face the bull or make an exception to your rule of the game of the walk ... you decide to pass him in the spirit of an escaping torero, or you make a rule to meet the danger. You take a bearing by your pocket-compass, and ascertain what tree or landmark you are naturally making for on the other side of the bull's field. And having assured yourself of that, you reach it by making a detour.

(Graham 1927)

Trespassing

There is a definite type of walker who loves trespassing for its own sake, and exults, as he climbs a fence or turns up a path marked 'Private,' in a vision of the landed aristocracy of England defied and impotent ... But like other unregenerate impulses, this carries its punishment with it. To indulge the love of trespassing involves ultimately making trespassing an end rather than a means, and this - like the twin passion for short-cuts as ends in themselves - is disastrous to walking.

Trespassing on high moral grounds has a further disadvantage that it leads to meticulous hair-splitting. I know walkers who think it right to trespass on the grounds of a large landowner, but not on those of a small landowner. They consequently draw a line at five acres or so, and have to consider, whenever trespassing is proposed, on which side of the line the field of action lies.

There are practical disadvantages, too - the keeper, flanked by dogs and fortified by a gun ... and there follows the mean and abject retreat to the nearest road with the vision of the landed aristocracy calm and triumphant.

(Sidgwick 1912)

The best method of coping with keepers is always to be in the front of and, if possible, leading a party. Persons so placed who meet a keeper can afford to ignore him and to proceed as if he were not there. For the keeper confronted with this situation will be torn different ways, on the one hand, he will wish to pursue you and curse you for your impertinence, on the other, he will see a considerable posse of people bearing down upon him from behind and will be moved to stay where he is and remonstrate with them. In my experience nine times out of ten he will do the latter. Thus the rearguard of the party draws the keeper's fire, while you in front pass serenely out of the infected area. But the rearguard cannot stay long, since they dare not run the risk of losing you, and with you their way.

Consequently, however great their fear of the keeper, they are obliged to defy him and to continue on their way, being impelled by a greater fear. They find you waiting for them some three fields ahead.

(Joad 1932)

To me, for many years, it was a necessity of life to interpolate gulps of fresh air between the periods of inhaling London fogs. When once beyond the "town" I looked out for notices that trespassers would be prosecuted. That gave a strong presumption that the trespass must have some attraction ... to me it was a reminder of the many delicious bits of walking which, even in the neighbourhood of London, await the man who has no superstitious reverence for legal rights. It is indeed surprising how many charming walks can be contrived by a judicious combination of a little trespassing with the rights of way happily preserved over so many commons and footpaths.

(Stephen 1901)

As ancient as the fields themselves, as securely based upon the ages and sanctified by the use of our fathers, the footpaths and field-tracks stand as the living embodiment of popular rights. Beside the way which the feet of generations have worn to church or inn, the loftiest dwellings and widest parks are mere parvenus. If the trespasser wishes to commit an act of symbolic defiance against the landed aristocracy ... he can tread the right-of-way which existed before they were thought of.

There is no surer guide for our rights than a steady and regular patrolling of our possessions.

(Sidgwick 1912)

Please trespass. The English game preserve is a citadel of woodland charm, and however precious, it has only one or two defenders easily eluded and, when met, most courteous to all but children and not very well dressed women. The burglar's must be a bewitching trade if we may judge by the pleasures of the trespasser's unskilled labour.

(Edward Thomas 1909)

But do we *really* want access for all or just for those sort of people of whom we generally approve? How many would secretly support 'Fred's Way'? Fred is a fisherman and lover of the countryside. He believes that all land and their waters should be privately owned and jealously keepered by bucolic bouncers armed with shotguns and rottweilers. In this way only those with sufficient ingenuity, determination or cheek would gain access. It would deter the casual family outing from dumping their litter, the throngs of earnest ramblers yodelling their way up the hillside and the myriad of other offences that Fred finds intrusive and annoying. He would also argue that trespassing gives an edge to the activity.

(Wilson 2002)

Getting lost

Variety can be obtained by losing the way - a half-conscious process, which in a sense can no more be done by deliberate purpose than falling in love. And yet a man can sometimes very wisely let himself drift, either into love or into the wrong path out walking. There is a joyous mystery in roaming on, reckless where you are going, into what valley, road or farm chance and the hour is guiding you. If the place is lonely and beautiful, and if you have lost all count of it upon the map, it may seem a fairy glen, a lost piece of old England that no surveyor would find though he searched for it a year. I scarcely know whether most to value this quality of aloofness and magic in country I have never seen before, and may never see again, or the familiar joys of Walking grounds where every tree and rock are rooted in the memories that make up my life.

(Trevelyan 1913)

Last Sunday morning, two schoolgirl daughters who wouldn't put any thick clothes on, and just wouldn't be told, and I, set out to climb a mountain [North Wales]. There was only one decent way up and that was along the ridge, and we swung up and along this ridge in great style and before one o'clock had reached the summit. But now we were lost in a cloud, couldn't see more than ten yards clearly, and out of this thick mist came a bitter, drenching rain, cold as January. It was all right while we were sheltering behind a rock and eating and drinking, but it was all wrong when we began our descent. We were wet through, shivering, and too anxious to get back home. Especially the two girls, who just wouldn't listen to the feeble protests of their father, who pointed out that he ought to have a map and compass, but hadn't, that descending a mountain consisting mostly of steep, slaty, wet slopes, in a thick fog, is no joke at all, and that we ought to be very wary and though our teeth might be chattering, we ought to take it easy, go a few steps at time, and not rush at it. But no, they said they remembered exactly which way we came up, though now we couldn't see anything, of course, and off they dashed, leaving me to follow them, bleating like an old sheep.

Well, I won't describe in detail how we completely lost ourselves in that chill, blank world, how we scrambled and slipped and peered over the edge of what looked like horrible precipices, and finally, after nearly breaking our necks a score of times, found ourselves past the worst slopes and descending into a valley. But then the mist lifted a little and we suddenly stopped congratulating ourselves, for we were near the edge of a lake, and we knew only too well that there was no lake in our valley, so that it was painfully obvious that we had come careering down the wrong side of the mountain and were miles and miles and miles from home.

Luckily we found a farmhouse near the lake, and inside it some very nice Welsh people - and the Welsh are very nice people - who've had the sense not to lose their time-old passion for sensible things like music and poetry - and so we were allowed to steam in front of a fire, given some hot tea, and at last driven over a bumpy little mountain road back home.

(Priestley 1940)

Sauntering

I have met with but one or two persons in the course of my life who understood the art of Walking, that is, of taking walks, - who had a genius, so to speak, for *sauntering*: which word is beautifully derived "from idle people who roved about the country, in the Middle Ages, and asked charity, under pretence of going *à la Sainte Terre*", to the Holy Land, till the children exclaimed, "There goes a *Sainte-Terrer*", a Saunterer. They who never go to the Holy Land in their walks, as they pretend, are indeed mere idlers and vagabonds, but they who do go there are saunterers in the good sense. He who sits still in a house all the time may be the greatest vagrant of all, but the saunterer is no more vagrant than the meandering river, which is all the while sedulously seeking the shortest course to the sea.

(Thoreau (1862) in Belloc 1911)

Walking away

Of the many ways of walking there is one way which is the greatest of all, and that is to walk away. There is a place above the Roman Wall beyond the River Tyne where one can do this thing. Behind one lies the hospitality and the human noise. Before one is the dead line of the road, and that complete emptiness of the moors as they rise up toward Cheviot on the one hand and Carter Fell upon the other. The earth is here altogether deserted and alone: you go out into it because it is your business to go: you are walking away ... and it is your business to leave all that you have known altogether behind you, and no man has eyes at the back of his head - go forward. Upon my soul I think that the greatest way of walking, now I consider the matter, or now that I have stumbled upon it, is walking away.

(Belloc 1911)

Night-walking

Then is the best yet to come, when the walk is carried on into the night, or into the long, silent, twilight hours which in the northern summer stand in night's place. Whether I am alone or with one fit companion, then most is the quiet soul awake, for then, the body, drugged with sheer health, is felt only as a part of the physical nature that surrounds it and to which it is indeed akin, while the mind's sole function is to be conscious of calm delight.

(Trevelyan 1913)

And what nights there are on the hills. The ash-sprays break up the low full moon into a flower of many sparks. The Downs are heaved up into the lighted sky - surely they have in their tranquillity as with a slowly taken breath. The moon is half-way up the sky and exactly over the centre of the long curve of Downs, just above them lies a long terrace of white cloud, and at their feet gleams a broad pond, the rest of the valley being utterly dark and undistinguishable, save a few scattered lamps and one near meadow that catches the moonlight so as to be transmuted to a lake.

(Edward Thomas 1909)

We now began to retrace out steps over the mountain. At first the mist appeared to be nearly cleared away. As we proceeded, however, large sheets began to roll up the mountain sides, and by the time we reached the summit we were completely shrouded in vapour. The night, however, was not very dark, and we found our way tolerably well, though once in descending I had nearly tumbled into the dingle, now on our left hand. The bushes and trees, seen indistinctly through the mist, had something of the look of goblins.

(Borrow 1862)

As I left the last house of the village I was not secure from loneliness, and when the road began to climb up the hill into the wild and the trees I was wondering how the night would pass.

With every step upward a greater mystery surrounded me. A few stars were out, and the brown night mist was creeping along the water below, but there was still light enough to see the road, and even to distinguish the bracken in the deserted hollows. The highway became little better than a lane, at the top of the hill it plunged under tall pines, and was vaulted over with darkness. The kingdoms that have no walls, and are built up of shadows, began to oppress me as the night hardened. Had I had companions, still we would only have spoken in a whisper, and in that dungeon of trees even my own self would not raise its voice within me.

(Belloc 1902)

The sun had been set some time, and we could perceive that the light was fading away from the coves of Helvellyn, but the lake under a luminous sky, was more brilliant than before. After tea at Patterdale, set out again, - a fine evening, the seven stars close to the mountain-top, all the stars seemed brighter than usual. The steeps were reflected in Brotherswater, and, above the lake appeared like enormous black perpendicular walls. The Kirkstone torrents had been swoln by the rain, and now filled the mountain pass with their roaring, which added greatly to the solemnity of our walk. Behind us, when we had climbed to a great height, we saw one light very distant in the vale, like a large red star - a solitary one in the gloomy region. The cheerfulness of the scene was in the sky above us. Reached home a little before midnight.

(Wordsworth, in Belloc 1911)

I was walking to Keswick, from my own cottage in Grasmere. The distance was thirteen miles, the time just nine o'clock, the night a cloudy moonlight, and intensely cold. I took the very greatest delight in these nocturnal walks through the silent valleys of Cumberland and Westmoreland, and often at hours far later than the present. What I liked in this solitary rambling was, to trace the course of the evening through its household hieroglyphics from the windows which I passed or saw: the blazing fires shining through the windows of houses, lurking in nooks far apart from neighbours, sometimes, in solitudes that seemed abandoned to the owl, to catch the sounds of household mirth, then, some miles further, to perceive the time of going to bed, then the gradual sinking to silence of the house, then the drowsy reign of the cricket, at intervals to hear church-clocks or a little solitary chapel-bell, under the brows of mighty hills, proclaiming the hours of the night, and flinging out their sullen knells over the graves where 'the rude forefathers of the hamlet slept' - where the strength and the loveliness of Elizabeth's time, or Cromwell's, and through so many fleeting generations that have succeeded, had long ago sunk to rest. Such was the sort of pleasure which I reaped in my nightly walks - of which, however, considering the suspicions of lunacy which it has sometimes awoke, the less I say, perhaps, the better.

(Thomas De Quincey 1834)

[at the foot of the Maloja Pass at night]

...I wanted to find the old Roman road up through the black pines. Wearing snow-shoes and a head-torch to read the compass I waded up through the forest till the light of the torch caught the first painted mark on a tree. The climb occupied half the night. In the deep snow and in the blackness of the forest, the path had entirely disappeared, and I could only make progress by leaving my rucksack and searching upward for the next paint-mark on a tree trunk, or other likely clues such as dips in the snow or linear clearings. Then I'd climb down again and recover my rucksack. Occasionally I caught a glimpse of headlights probing the icy road far below. Few night climbs had given me as much pleasure.

(Crane 1997)

My rucksack felt a ton weight as I staggered along the road ... It was too dark to read the map ... I became ravenous and had to think myself into a trance to rise above it. I hadn't eaten all day, saving myself for the evening. My feet got to the stage where they became displaced persons, great lumps moving stiffly forward, not knowing where or how but knowing that stopping would mean being unable ever to start again. I realised almost I was enjoying the agony of being absolutely exhausted, of being an automaton, but I couldn't be, so I kept telling myself. I counted trees and shadows and car lights in the distance, tricking myself that I was moving and that I hadn't been sentenced to mark time for ever. What I wanted most in the world was a hot bath.

(Hunter Davies 1993)

CHAPTER 6

DID YOU HAVE A REST?

But I had done too much in the night march, for my next day was a day without salt, and in it appreciation left me. And this breakdown of appreciation was due to what I did not know at the time to be fatigue, but to what was undoubtedly a deep inner exhaustion ... All that day was destined to be covered, so far as my spirit was concerned, with a motionless lethargy. Nothing seemed properly to interest or to concern me, and not till evening was I visited by any muse. Even my pain (which was now dull and chronic) was no longer a subject for my entertainment, and I suffered from an uneasy isolation that had not the merit of sharpness and was no spur to the mind. I had the feeling that every one I might see would be a stranger, and that their language would be unfamiliar to me, and this, unlike most men who travel, I had never felt before ... I had marched 180 miles. It was no wonder that on this eighth day I was oppressed and that all the light long I drank no good wine, met no one to remember well, nor sang any songs ... I say a day without salt. A trudge. The air was ordinary, the colours common, men, animals, and trees indifferent. Something had stopped working.

(Belloc 1902)

It is good to take a whole day off in the middle of a walking tour. It is easy to get stale, yet it is a pity to shorten a good walk for fear of being tired next day. One day off in a well-chosen hamlet, in the middle of a week's "hard", is often both necessary to the pleasure of the next three days, and good in itself. All day long, as we lie perdu in wood or field, we have perfect laziness and perfect health. The body is asleep like a healthy infant - or, if it must be doing for one hour of the blessed day, let it scramble a little, while the powers of mind and soul are at their topmost strength and yet are not put forth, save intermittently and casually, like a careless giant's hand. Our modern life requires such days of "anti-worry", and they are only to be obtained in perfection when the body has been walked to a standstill.

(Trevelyan 1913)

For the five hottest hours we should have grunted and sweated up a vertical mile of turf and shale, boulder and snow, bent under our fardels of food and camp kit and fuel, maledictions no doubt on our lips and deep joy in our hearts.

There like the gods we should lie at our ease, with twilight Europe laid out below us.

(Montague 1924)

[in the Pyrenees]

I was always reassured when the ebb and flow of human affairs contrived to make unlikely connections, believing in the existence of these slender threads helped me to feel part of the greater whole, less left out, less alone. Sitting on a polished rock, I liked to think that mine was just another in an eternal chronology of aching arses to have chosen that spot for a rest. The mountains were dotted with these nodes of human inter-connection, from modern sites like the Voyageurs to the seat-worn slabs that have been rested upon since the hunters moved in behind the shrinking ice sheets.

(Crane 1997)

I now understand the true significance of the term "peripatetic philosopher." A philosopher who walks about possesses twice the power of one who remains glued to his chair. Walking stimulates the brain like a tonic, provided that the philosopher knows when to halt and take his rest. Whenever a man tells me with pride in his voice that he has tramped thirty miles in the day, I shun meeting him at the evening meal, for I know that he has stupefied himself and become an automaton. Walking is enjoyable when one punctuates its rhythm by a series of short pauses, for we should remember that if walking is rhythm, resting is melody.

When I am striding forward, I carry on imaginary conversations with all kinds of people real and imaginary, I laugh and gesticulate, I blaze with indignation and swipe about with my stick, I deliver speeches, I reply to taunts, I can become more tender and impassioned than in real life, because I am alone and unobserved. When a shady fig-tree or a grassy knoll with tiny spring bubbling up through clover tempts me to rest, I can dismiss with a wave of the hand the companions of my thoughts and sink down to rest in the shade. I know that as soon as I lie down on the mossy bank, my mind will rest and my senses become lulled by the murmuring water.

(Starkie 1936)

As I lay so leisurely watching the sun, it occurred to me that there was no reason why man should not give up quests when he wanted to - he was not fixed on a definite course like the sun.

(Graham 1912)

The sight of the resting country does his spirit good. There is something better than music in the wide unusual silence, and it disposes him to amiable thoughts, like the sound of a little river or the warmth of sunlight.

(Stevenson 1896)

Nor is it only the countryside that I need, it must be the English countryside. Time and again I have been to beautiful places abroad, the Italian Lakes, the Alps, the Mediterranean Coast, the Pyrenees, and been homesick for the English country. It is not that I do not know these places to be beautiful, merely that I do not feel at home in them. The eternal blue sky welcomed for a few days, is felt as a nuisance by the end of a week, the flowers are not English flowers, the grass is coarse and sparse, the rocks jagged and harsh, there is nowhere to lie about. The English country is unequalled in the facilities it provides for lounging and lying about.

(Joad 1932)

[on the Icknield Way]

Looking about for somewhere to rest, I found it under a bank. Now of all the objects on which men have reclined, none is more comfortable than a well-grooved grassy bank that has been dried by sun and wind. So there I lay, full length on the turf, with my head supported by a pillow of primroses, and in that luxury I forgot the past, dismissed the future, and allowed the present to seep through the pores and then into the brain, or the intellect, or the soul, or whatever else you care to call that part of us which appears to be the seat of self-consciousness.

(Peel 1976)

I allowed myself two days to tramp the distance of sixty kilometres. So I started off one morning full of determination to walk my thirty kilometres before resting by the way. The majority of pedestrian travellers set out full of confidence in their powers of resistance. Oh yes, they could continue until kingdom come, for the air is nippy and the sun is shining. But search for them after eight or nine kilometres and you would find them lying on their back by the side of the road with cap pulled down over their eyes, snoring beatifically as if they had reached the end of their trek. So it was with me. I made a rule for myself that I would rest after every five kilometres, but I found that the rule did not work, for as soon as I lay down by the ditch to rest I fell asleep for about an hour. When I woke up and started afresh it took me two or three kilometres to get rid of my yawns.

(Starkie 1936)

The tendency for walkers and climbers to admire the view is always most marked in the early hours of the day. There are base creatures who insinuate that the object of such halts is not the view at all, but a desire for rest, and in fairness to this theory it must be admitted that stops become infrequent after the party has warmed to its task or sees the end in sight, whereas early in the morning its members are collectively and individually struck by the beauty of the landscape and are forced to admire or photograph it at intervals of ten minutes. If a day ever comes when all hikers and mountaineers are fighting fit, the manufacturers of film will feel the draught.

(Borthwick 1939)

The virtue to be envied in tramping is that of being able to live by the way. In that indeed does the gentle art of tramping consist. If you do not live by the way, there is nothing gentle about it. It is then a stunt, a something done to make a dull person ornamental. I listen with pained reluctance to those who claim to have walked forty or fifty miles a day. But it is a pleasure to meet a man who has learned the art of going slowly, the man who disdained not to linger in the happy morning hours, to listen, to watch, to exist.

The noontide meal is a siesta which can be very pleasantly prolonged. It only takes half an hour to make the fire and boil the pot, but you have left no "back in half-an-hour" notice in any town. The grand desideratum is to have found an agreeable spot.

"We can put in forty minutes here!" - "My friend, hours!" There is a joyous, light-green glittering sleep between the hours of two and four, hours not lost nor to be missed in the temporal economy of the tramp.

You continue the way with more camaraderie, doing an indolent eight or nine miles before sundown. The afternoon walk is likely to be different from the morning one, you are less eager, more passive and indulgent and sociable.

(Graham 1927)

It was one of those delicious ends to perfect days which give a man the feeling of having accomplished something, but by no means compel him to inquire what. The road still possessed the hills even when it was enclosed on both sides, for it kept broad margins, the hedges were low between it and the grass or corn land, and it mounted higher and higher.

(Edward Thomas 1913)

As the day goes on, the traveller becomes more and more incorporated with the material landscape, and the open-air drunkenness grows upon him with great strides, until he posts along the road, and sees everything about him, as in a cheerful dream.

(Stevenson 1889)

Indeed the only reason, other than weakness of the flesh, for not always walking until late at night, is the joy of making a leisurely occupation of the hamlet that chance or whim has selected for the night's rest. There is much merit in the stroll after supper, hanging contemplative at sunset over the little bridge, feeling at one equally with the geese there on the common and with the high gods at rest on Olympus. After a day's walk everything has twice its usual value. Food and drink become subjects for epic celebration ... greed is sanctified by hunger and health.

(Trevelyan 1913)

You come to a milestone on a hill, or some place where deep ways meet under trees, and off goes the knapsack, and down you sit to smoke a pipe in the shade. You sink into yourself, and the birds come round and look at you, and your smoke dissipates upon the afternoon under the blue dome of heaven, and the sun lies warm upon your feet, and the cool air visits your neck and turns aside your open shirt. If you are not happy, you must have an evil conscience.

But it is at night, and after dinner, that the best hour comes. There are no such pipes to be smoked as those that follow a good day's march ... if you wind up the evening with grog, you will own there was never such grog ... if you read a book - and you will never do so save by fits and starts - you find the language strangely racy and harmonious, words take a new meaning, single sentences possess the ear for half an hour together, and the writer endears himself to you, at every page, by the nicest coincidence of sentiment. It seems as if it were a book you had written yourself in a dream.

You lean from the window, your last pipe reeking whitely into the darkness, your body full of delicious pains, your mind enthroned in the seventh circle of content, when suddenly the mood changes, the weather-cock goes about, and you ask yourself one question more: whether for the interval, you have been the wisest philosopher or the most egregious of donkeys? Human experience is not yet able to reply, but at least you have had a fine moment, and looked down upon all the kingdoms of the earth. And whether it was wise or foolish, to-morrow's travel will carry you, body and mind, into some different parish of the infinite.

(Stevenson 1889)

A characteristic of misadventures is that their sequels are often heaven-sent, the calm after the storm brings pleasures whose intensity is sharpened by the ghastliness of that which went before. I woke in Cain warm, dry and safe with the rest of my life stretched ahead like an eternal summer.

The problem with hot water, good food and utilities such as tables and chairs ...was that their intoxicating sensuousness subverted the will to return to itineracy.

(Crane 1997)

[Rannoch Moor]

So entranced were Dougie and I by the panorama unfolded to our gaze by the mere flicking aside of the tent door, that it seemed to us sheer sacrilege, bad taste, and a casting away of the gifts of providence to arise from our beds before nine o'clock in the morning, though we had wakened at eight. It was a perfect day. The morning mist was rising like steam from the surface of Loch Laidon, and in the bracken tangle before us a thousand spiders' webs were spread like lace, dew-covered and glittering in the sun. A branch of scarlet rowan berries overhung the tent door, and the sky, crisp blue above, shaded by imperceptible degrees of grey down to the smoky mountains on the horizon. Such were the blandishments of bed, loch, mountains, moor, sausages and honey that ten o'clock had come and gone before we had the tent stowed away and the first mile behind us.

(Borthwick 1939)

Sleeping out

I am prejudiced in favour of that kind of tramping where one sleeps out. Strictly speaking, if one sleeps in hotels or houses, it is not a tramp but a walking tour.

(Graham 1927)

For in Sleep a man utterly sinks down in proportion as it is deep and good into the centre of things and becomes one with that from which he came, drawing strength not only by negation from repose, but in some way positive from the being of his mother which is the earth. Some say that sleep is better near against the ground on this account, and all men know that sleep in wild places and without cover is the surest and the best.

(Belloc 1912a)

Sleep under the sky is seldom that utter withdrawal from life. Through some sort of film, some sort of feeler within you is still aware of the rhythmic murmur of existence, some unspecified part of your system keeps watch and reports to the rest that all's well.

(Montague 1924)

The most glorious and wonderful nights I ever had were almost sleepless ones, spent looking at the stars and tasting the new sensations ... even the cold untires and refreshes. Then, even if one lies awake, the night passes with extraordinary rapidity. It is always a marvel to me how long the day seems by comparison with the night when I sleep out of doors. A sleepless night in a house is an eternity, but it is only a brief interlude under the stars.

(Graham 1912)

[an undergraduate at Oxford c. 1910]

... that heavenly walk from Cumnor village down the Long Leys to Bablock Hythe. Once I spent the night at the Bablock Hythe inn - it was small and simple then - just across the water. It was the first time I had ever gone to the country for a night alone. I was steeped in the literature of walking and expected to enjoy profound spiritual experiences. In fact, I was lonely, bored and a little scared. It was one of the first occasions on which I discovered the difference between literature and life.

(Joad 1946)

Depressed by the great indoors scene, still eager for new adventures, we tackled Olympia's sixteenth Annual Camping and Outdoor Life Exhibition [1974]. With his Durapegs, Foldecarrier, Portashower and Mini-Sweep, the modern camper can stick to a safe Polywarm, Instaflam, Maxicool, Tuck-Away, Charglow world without ever really feeling that he has abandoned the armchair.

Camping equipment makers seem devoted to excruciating trade marks, and making the flit from camp site to camp site in search of Europleasure as much like staying at home as possible. The apotheosis of it all is the announcement of 'the answer to a long-felt want in the camping world'. It's a double camp bed, 'with specially designed head board if desired ... erection is simple even in the dark'.

(*Observer* 6 January 1974)

Beginner camper asks experienced camper for the secret of putting up a tent in the rain: 'nothing special - just quicker'.

(Tom Patterson)

I halted for the night at the foot of a knoll where there was a small rustic graveyard nestling peacefully in the moonlight. At the back of a big sheltering tomb-stone I made a fire of twigs and prepared to bivouack in Gypsy style in this desolate spot, feeling sure that no one would come to disturb me in a cemetery. I had some cheese and bread in my rucksac and my wine-skin was full. As the night continued and the fire burnt low I began to feel acute melancholy and loneliness. I was sorry that I had chosen a graveyard for bivouacking ground, for graveyards brought thoughts of Vampires and Werewolves to the mind. I tried to dispel this attack of the shivers by music, but my violin sounded harsh and discordant like a *danse macabre*.

When I settled down ... the night became for me a series of hopeless struggles with mosquitoes and every other species of stinging insect. As long as the fire was burning merrily the insects gave me a wide berth, but later on in the shadows of the night I heard the ominous high note like the tuning of countless violins by a phantom orchestra and the hordes began their descent upon my unarmed flesh. Soon I felt my face swell under their attacks and sleep became an impossibility ... another distressing feature of outdoor sleeping was the prevalence of such crawling beasts as earwigs and woodlice, not to mention the sprightly flea. When I started to doze in a short period of respite from the mosquito orchestra, I felt an ominous tickling sensation on my neck. I found that a legion of ants was advancing in extended order over my body.

(Starkie 1933)

Mountains and valleys lay within me, robed in sunny or cloudy days or marching in the majesty of storm. I had inbreathed their mystery and outbreathed it as my own...Beauteous plains had tempted, mysterious dark forces lured me, and I had loved them and given them habitation in my being. My soul had been wedded to the great strong sun and it had slumbered under the watchful stars.

(Graham 1912)

[camping on the fringe of the Moor of Rannoch]

It was a night of black and silver, with a full moon sailing over the mountains and shedding a track of light across the loch at our feet. The night was still, and threw into sharp relief the small sounds which floated to us over the loch, and the crackles and explosions of the fire we had made from the ruins of a rotten birch, and when the fire died in a bed of glowing ash the small sounds came into their own, so that we could hear, for our ears were stretched to hear them, every flicker of the wings of the solitary bat flipping back and forth overhead, and the distant roar of a stag. The scraps of the meal were scattered around us. We were fed and replete. Wood smoke was sharp in our nostrils. The Milky Way arched over us. It was a night to dream about.

(Borthwick 1939)

The wind among the trees was my lullaby. Sometimes it sounded for minutes together with a steady even rush, not rising nor abating, and again it would swell and burst like a great crashing breaker, and the trees would patter me all over with big drops from the rain of the afternoon. Night after night, in my own bedroom in the country, I have given ear to this perturbing concert of the wind among the woods, but whether it was a difference in the trees, or the lie of the ground, or because I was myself outside and in the midst of it, the fact remains that the wind sang to a different tune among these woods of Gévaudan.

(Stevenson 1896)

Sleeping by a river there is the sound all night of faint human voices, too far away to make out what they are saying.

(Tom Patterson)

There was a quality of tranquillity in these Carpathian backwaters that I'd not found in western Europe. Here, you could lie back and look at the stars knowing that the winking lights of an airliner would not break the spell, here, the horizons never carried the orange fur of city lights. This was peace at its purest, a peace which - in the world where I came from - was no longer regarded as a human essential.

(Crane 1997)

The night darkened ... feeling very wakeful I pushed on up the valley under great woods of pines, and at last, diverging up a little path, I settled on a clump of trees sheltered and, as I thought, warm, and lay down there to sleep till morning, but, on the contrary, I lay awake a full hour in the fragrance and on the level carpet of the pine needles looking up through the dark branches at the waning moon, which had just risen, and thinking of how suitable were pine-trees for a man to sleep under ... here was a warm place under the pines where I could rest in great comfort on pine needles still full of the day, a covering for the beasts underground that love an even heat - the best of floors for a tired man.

(Belloc 1902)

Came dawn and what the Irish would call a fine soft morning, that's to say it pelted down. Stretching out I put my feet into a small but very cold pond. During the night, a little rivulet had trickled in and hadn't been able to trickle out. All my underclothes were soaking wet together with several maps, a book on the flora of the Alps and the toe-end of a heavily quilted sleeping bag. I'm relating all this dispassionately as if it were the sort of thing I have grown accustomed to. It's what I remember when people say how nice it must be to sleep out in the open.

(Hillaby 1972)

One night I had gone into the fields, and, getting together a dozen or more wheatsheaves, proceeded to build a house with them, making a dry floor on the damp earth, with walls to shelter from the wind, and a roof to shelter from the dew, leaving just space enough at one end to admit my body. I had been in here comfortable and warm for some time, when it began to rain. In half an hour the rain leaked in large drops through the roof, and in less than an hour these drops had become streams. There was nothing to do but to remain, for it was now too dark to seek shelter. For ten hours it rained incessantly, and I was literally wet to the skin, and no drier than a person immersed in water - not wet to the skin as people commonly express it when they are damp after a few showers. I was nothing daunted, looking on this as one of the many experiences that I was compelled to undergo. The next morning I chose a secluded spot in the open air, so as to lie down where the sun, coming out warm and strong, would dry me while I slept. Two or three times have I suffered in this way, but have never felt any ill effects after.

(Davies 1908)

After an apprehensive moment in the fading light on the edge of cliff, I remembered something the tramp had told me and gently kicked a cow to her feet. The animal rose from the dew-wet grasses, rumbling indignantly, leaving a warm, dry patch, just about the size of a groundsheet. I put the tent down there and slept like a child.

(Hillaby 1968)

When darkness came, full of moths and beetles, I was too weary to put up the tent. So I lay myself down in the middle of a field and stared up at the brilliant stars. I was oppressed by the velvety emptiness of the world and the swathes of soft grass I lay on. Then the fumes of the night finally put me to sleep - my first night without a roof or bed.

I was woken soon after midnight by drizzling rain on my face, the sky black and the stars all gone. Two cows stood over me, windily sighing, and the wretchedness of that moment haunts me still. I crawled into a ditch and lay awake till dawn, soaking alone in that nameless field. But when the sun rose in the morning, the feeling of desolation was over. Birds sang, and the grass steamed warmly. I got up and shook myself, ate a piece of cheese, and turned again to the south.

(Laurie Lee 1969)

There are, as perhaps the reader knows by experience, no jaguars in Wales - nor pumas - nor anacondas - nor (generally speaking) any Thugs. What I feared most, but perhaps only through ignorance of zoology, was lest, whilst my sleeping face was upturned to the stars, some one of the many little Brahminical-looking cows on the Cambrian hills might poach her foot into the centre of my face. I do not suppose any fixed hostility of that nature to English faces in Welsh cows.

(De Quincey 1802 in Belloc 1911)

[Wainwright on Scafell Pike]

I would say that the most intense experiences have occurred during nights spent on the fells. Occasionally (not often, and only in Summer) I have bivouacked alone in high places, these occasions remain vivid in my memory! Nobody who has not done it can imagine the splendours of sunset and sunrise from the summits, the eerie stillness of the hours of darkness, the joy of being on the tops at dawn when the larks are rising. I recommend this to everyone who loves the fells, but I recommend company to all but guide-book writers.

(Hunter Davies 2004)

On leaving a perfect isolated camp-site - as it might be on a grassy ledge by Randale Beck, with waterfalls above and below - it seems essential to leave an inconspicuous marker, an altar-stone to thank the gods. This may take the form of a flat stone wedged upright, surrounded by a ring of smaller stones. The upright should be aligned to the rising sun - to the point where the sun first appears in a dip in the hills - 'camper's east'.

(Tom Patterson)

At the top of the woods, which do not climb very high upon this cold ridge, I struck leftward by a path among the pines, until I hit on a dell of green turf, where a streamlet made a little spout over some stones to serve me for a water-tap. The trees were not old, but they grew thickly round the glade: there was no outlook, except north-eastward upon distant hill-tops, or straight upward to the sky, and the encampment felt secure and private like a room ... as soon as the sun went down, I pulled my cap over my eyes and fell asleep.

Night is a dead monotonous period under a roof, but in the open world it passes lightly, with its stars and dews and perfumes, and the hours are marked by changes in the face of Nature. What seems a kind of temporal death to people choked between walls and curtains, is only a light and living slumber to the man who sleeps afield. All night long he can hear Nature breathing deeply and freely, even as she takes her rest she turns and smiles, and there is one stirring hour unknown to those who dwell in houses, when a wakeful influence goes abroad over the sleeping hemisphere, and all the outdoor world are on their feet. It is then that the cock first crows, not this time to announce the dawn, but like a cheerful watchman speeding the course of night. Cattle awake on the meadows, sheep break their fast on dewy hillsides, and change to a new lair among the ferns, and houseless men, who have lain down with the fowls, open their dim eyes and behold the beauty of the night.

I had been most hospitably received and punctually served in my green caravanserai. The room was airy, the water excellent, and the dawn had called me to a moment. I say nothing of the tapestries or the inimitable ceiling, nor yet of the view which I commanded from the windows, but I felt I was in someone's debt for all this liberal entertainment. And so it pleased me, in a half-laughing way, to leave pieces of money on the turf as I went along, until I had left enough for my night's lodging.

(Stevenson 1896)

[following Stevenson's footsteps]

I slept out that night under an outcrop of pines, facing east on a slight incline, with the lights of Costaros far away to my left. The turf was springy, and the pine needles seemed to discourage insects. As I lay in my bag, a number of late rooks came winging in out of the gloaming and settled in the pine branches, chuckling to each other. They gave me a sense of companionship, even security: nothing could move up through the trees below me without disturbing them. Once or twice I croaked up at them (it was the wine), and they croaked back: "Tais-toi, tais-toi." This night I fell asleep quickly. Only once, waking, I drank two ice-cold mouthfuls of water from my can and, leaning back, saw the Milky Way astonishingly bright through the pine tops, and felt something indescribable - like falling upwards into someone's arms.

(Holmes 1985)

[following Stevenson]

So many self-conscious Stevensonians have already poked about in this wood that I half expected to bump into knots of young men puffing meerschaums, with TWAD open on page 172 and clutching twitching divining rods. I found the dell, or at least I found a dell which would do. The young trees surrounding his camp-site were now statuesque Scots pine and in the calm of the evening I knew why Stevenson had spliced into his chapter the sequestered-bower quote from Paradise Lost.[1]

Dawn broke and I lay in my sleeping-bag postponing the moment when I would have to pull on my wet trousers.

(Crane 1997)

---

[1] In shadier bower
More sacred and sequestered, though but feigned,
Pan or Sylvanus never slept, nor Nymph
For Faunus haunted

CHAPTER 7
WHAT DID YOU TAKE WITH YOU?

There are at least two moments in which equipment will be charged with the full force of the poetic current. One is at the very beginning of a walk, when everything is fresh and clean, when shirts are cool and unrumpled, and boots are new-greased, and the walking stick lies cold and hard in the hand, and the knapsack sits on the shoulders like a bird new-poised and unfamiliar with its perch ... we feel that we are armed for the combat with time and space and wind and weather and mental depression and abstract thinking.

The other moment comes later, when we are some days upon our way. Boots have grown limp: clothes have settled into natural skin-like rumples, the stick is warm and smooth to our touch: the map slips easily in and out of the pocket, lucubrated by dog's-ears: every article in the knapsack has found its natural place, and the whole has settled on to our shoulders as its home. The equipment is no longer an external armour of which we are conscious: it is part of ourselves that has come through the combat with us, and is indissolubly linked with its memories. At the start this coat was a glorious thing to face the world in: now it is merely an outer skin. At the start the stick was mine: now it is myself.

(Sidgwick 1912)

Something hugely attractive stands out from any sort of gear which has been hard used but well cared for. The frays, the repairs, the pattern of stains on that battered pack are the high tide marks of adventure.

(Hillaby 1976)

During the first day or so of any tour there are moments of bitterness, when the traveller feels more than coldly towards his knapsack, when he is half in a mind to throw it bodily over the hedge ... And yet it soon acquires a property of easiness. It becomes magnetic, the spirit of the journey enters into it. And no sooner have you passed the straps over your shoulder than the lees of sleep are cleared from you, you pull yourself together with a shake, and fall at once into your stride.

(Stevenson 1889)

Now that at last I was on the open road, I was carrying my stuff with me in a rucksack. The last time I'd travelled with a rucksack was as a student. In those days I made my wife, a big strapping lass, carry the rucksack except through villages when, for the sake of appearances, I carried it.

(Hunter Davies 1993)

I incline to the view, never before expressed, that a rucksack is not at all necessary on a walking tour. How can some hikers enjoy themselves beneath the weight of their huge, fifty-pound burdens completely passes my comprehension. I have had expeditions in the Lake District without a pack, and gone short of nothing. I take a light raincoat or cape, always, but never a change of clothes, nor an extra shirt, nor pyjamas. The clothes I wear when I set off must suffice: if they get wet, it is unfortunate for walking in wet raiment is unpleasant, but they have never failed to get dry afterwards. Pyjamas are, of course, a nuisance at all times and have no saving grace. A pair of slippers is a comfort, and additional socks are essential, but these will slip easily into a pocket.

On this occasion my rucksack contained four maps, the one in use being carried in my pocket. I had a toothbrush and a safety razor, a bottle of Indian ink and a pen, pencils and a rubber and a few postcards ... all told, the entire contents of my rucksack would weigh less than two pounds, so that I was free to square my shoulders and stride out as quickly as I pleased.

(Wainwright 1986)

[A Mountain Walk Across Europe]

I had one set of clothes. I lived in a pair of cotton trousers and a cotton shirt with two breast pockets in which I carried my passport, money and compass. For evenings I had a warm jacket and for bad weather a windproof cotton coat. For cold nights I carried a set of thermal underwear.

After some deliberation I had increased the size of my medical kit from three sticking plasters to four.

(Crane 1977)

[Wainwright's advice on clothing]

.... is to ignore all advice. 'Comfort is the thing. Wear shoes or sandals or go barefoot if those suit you better than boots. Comfort includes keeping warm and dry but ways of achieving it differ widely. The most ghastly apparitions appear on fells. If sheep didn't have such good manners they would laugh their heads off.

You see hikers setting forth for a day on the hills burdened as though they were starting a six-month expedition to Antarctica. They are grim and anguished when they ought to be carefree and smiling.'

(Hunter Davies 2000)

[Coleridge touring Cumberland in 1802 - he climbed Scafell alone]

... taking in his 'net knapsack' a shirt, a cravat, two pairs of stockings, tea, sugar, pens and paper, his night-cap, and a book of German poetry wrapped in green oilskin. For staff he carried the handle of the family broom, removed amid the protests of his womenfolk.

(Marples 1959)

[Ellen Weeton on Snowdon in 1825]

... a small slouch straw hat, a grey stuff jacket and petticoat. In one hand she carried a parasol and in the other a white net bag containing a map, a memorandum book, three boiled eggs and a crust of bread.

'The precipice, on my right and left both, was too much for my head to bear, on my right, if I slipped ever so little, nothing could save me, and it looked like an eternity of falling, it seemed to my giddy head half a mile down' ... but she pulled down her bonnet over her right cheek 'to hoodwink me on that side', and passed safely across.

(Marples 1959)

... a clear frosty November morning, the scene an open heath, having for the background that huge chain of mountains in which Skiddaw and Saddleback are pre-eminent ... that *blind road* ... the track so slightly marked by the passengers' footsteps that it can but be traced by a slight shade of verdure from the darker heath around it, and, being only visible to the eye when at some distance, ceases to be distinguished while the foot is actually treading it - along this faintly-traced path advances the object of our present narrative. Nothing can be on a more reduced scale than his travelling equipment. A volume of Shakespeare in each pocket, a small bundle with a change of linen slung across his shoulders, an oaken cudgel in his hand, complete our pedestrian's accommodations.

(Scott 1857)

[for 'a pedestrian tour in South Wales' at the end of October]

I bought a small leather satchel with a lock and key, in which I placed a white linen shirt, a pair of worsted stockings, a razor, and a prayer-book. Along with it I bought a leather strap with which to sling it over my shoulder, I got my boots new soled, my umbrella, which was rather dilapidated, mended, put twenty sovereigns into my purse, and then said I am all right.

(Borrow 1862)

[on the Path to Rome across the Alps]

I had, in a small bag or pocket slung over my shoulder, a large piece of bread, half a pound of smoked ham, a sketch-book, two Nationalist papers, and a quart of the wine of Brulé - which is the most famous wine in the neighbourhood of the garrison, yet very cheap.

(Belloc 1902)

... blankets and socks, a coffee-pot and a frying-pan ... knife and fork and spoon, skillet, towels which we sewed into sacks, mugs, and what was labelled "The Mystic Mit - the greatest discovery since soap for cleaning pots and pans."

(Graham, 1922)

I was nineteen years old, still soft at the edges, but with a confident belief in good fortune. I carried a small rolled-up tent, a violin in a blanket, a change of clothes and a tin of treacle biscuits. I was excited, vain-glorious, knowing I had far to go, but not, as yet, how far.

(Laurie Lee 1969)

[in the Pyrenees]

The first question asked by an Englishman about to attempt fresh journeys will be what things he must take with him from England. My answer is. Two things only, his woollen clothing and a pannikin ... everything upon you should be of wool, except your boots. The pannikin has a spirit lamp which just fits into the interior, with a metal receptacle for methylated spirits ... the advantage lies entirely in its compactness. Weight counts. Every ounce counts when you are knocked out on the third day, and the third day - the forty-eighth hour of losing your way and of missing human succour - may happen to you oftener than you think.

Where are you to get the rest of your kit, and of what kind will it be? You must purchase it in any one of the towns in the foothills, and the nearer to the mountains you buy it, the better for you, since the further out you are upon the plains, the more they look upon you, with justice, as a fool who will buy bad or useless material at too dear a rate, and lose, waste, or destroy it in a very few days, a mere tourist to be fleeced.

The things you will need are four: first you will need a gourd, next sandals, next a sack (with a pound and a half of bread, sausage of salt pig flavoured with garlic ("wonderfully sustaining"), three or four dozen Maggi capsules for making "a hot and comforting soup", one pint of methylated spirits, matches and a length of candle) and lastly a blanket.

The gourd is a leather bottle made of goat's skin with the hair inside ... it is designed by Heaven to prevent any man abusing God's great gift of wine, for the goat's hair inside gives to wine so appalling a taste that a man will only take of it exactly what is necessary for his needs.

As to the sack, nothing is more difficult than to advise upon this matter. Some men to be happy must carry a block and pencils, and colours, and brushes. Others cannot live without combs. Nothing is really necessary besides bread and meat.

(Belloc 1909)

There goes the author ... ready for the Black Mountains, with a bag full of purple plums, and a crinkly brown pork pie and some sandwiches. There is a compass and some maps in the knapsack, and a couple of cameras swing in leather cases from opposite shoulders, one takes monochrome photographs and the other takes colour. A broad green visor shields his eyes from the upland glare, and soft rubber heels on his steel-capped shoes take the shock of the hard surfaces and protect his spinal vertebrae. His equipment has been collected to the last detail, nothing has been forgotten. There is a fine green filter for his Zeiss lens, an orange one to use in the mountains, a yellow one for the skies, a tripod, a walking stick, a police whistle and a fly whisk.

What a glorious day!

(Potts 1949)

It is wonderful how much you can carry when it is for pleasure.

(Graham 1927)

Maps and guides

There are the inexperienced, who cannot read a map, and the complete nogs who have never seen one.

(Wainwright 1973)

When the inspiration for wandering and tramping has come we realise what a boon maps are, we come to love them, as inseparable companions ... you unfold them in the desert, you lie on them, you crawl about with a magnifying glass examining their small print and the lost names of villages in smudged mountain-ranges. You learn by the scale what the length of your thumb or little finger means in kilometres and miles. You survey with a curious joy the dotted line of your peregrinations up to that point.

(Graham 1927)

One of the first ideas that come to a man when he thinks of wandering about an unknown country is that it will be more fun if he does not take a map. There are places of which this is true, you discover for yourself, and it is more exciting.

(Belloc 1909)

I have used a good many maps in my time, largely to avoid the towns, but I confess that I prefer to do without them and to go, if I have some days before me, guided by the hills or the sun or a stream - or, if I have one day only, in a rough circle, trusting, by taking a series of turnings to the left or a series to the right, to take much beauty by surprise and to return at last to my starting-point. On a dull day or a cloudy night I have often no knowledge of the points of the compass. I never go out to see anything.

(Edward Thomas 1909)

Give me a map to look at, and I am content. Give me a map of country I know, and I am comforted: I live my travels over again, step by step, I recall the journeys I have made, half-forgotten incidents spring vividly to mind, and again I can suffer and rejoice at experiences which are once more made very real. Old maps are old friends, understood only by the man with whom they have travelled the miles. Nobody could read my maps as I do. Lend a book to a friend and he can enjoy it and miss nothing of its story: lend him a map, and he cannot even begin to read the tale it has to tell. For maps are personal things which books are not. The appeal of an old map is to the memory, an old map spread across my knees closes my eyes. The older, the more tattered it is, the greater my affection for it. I recall our adventures together in storm and sunshine, an occasion, perhaps, when it slipped from my pocket and I searched my tracks anxiously, as for a lost companion, until it was found, an occasion, perhaps, when the mist was thick, and instinct and the map urged different ways, and I followed the map and came to safe ground again. Ah yes, maps are grand companions. I have thrown books away, but never a map.

Give me a map of country I do not know, even of country I shall never know, and it has the power to thrill and excite me. No book has such an appeal to the imagination. A new map means new routes to plan, and ever so carefully, for the ground is strange and regard must be given to contours and watersheds and passes. My map becomes not a square of coloured linen, but a picture of the country itself. That blue daub becomes a glittering lake fringed with pine woods, the black specks a clustered village set amongst rich meadows in a corner of the valley, the faint red lines a steep mountain face soaring majestically into the heavens. My route is planned to the last detail, altered again and again, it is an ambitious programme, for there are no ties of home to bind me and limit the objective, expense is nothing. It is finished, it is perfect. It doesn't matter that I will never be able to do it. My pleasure has been great, yet, sadly enough, it is a pleasure shared by the very few. Map-lovers are scarce, book-lovers many, yet I think the reward of the lover of maps is far and away the greater. If it is ever my lot to be cast away on a desert island, let it be with an atlas and a one inch map of the Lake District.

(Wainwright 1986)

[Walker Miles, the author of *Field Path Rambles* and other guide-books for walking in the home counties]

With consummate care and precision he set himself to select from the vast complex of footpaths the best and most interesting, to weave them into continuous walks bearing a practical relation to the facilities for railway travel and food supply, and then, by instructions which even the most careless could hardly mistake, to lay them open to his followers. We can picture him with his note-book and compass, piecing together the stray and apparently purposeless fragments of path which abound in our country, harking back, altering, revising, adding touches of detail for the guidance of the inexperienced, suppressing all superfluity, sparing no pains in his effort to spread the good knowledge, to reveal the vast open space for enjoyment and recreation, and, in a very real sense, to restore England to the English.

He himself has gone to return no more, and only his works remain. But I like to think that somewhere on the Elysian plain, where prophet and hero and poet tread together down the well-worn paths, a single figure quests somewhat aside, writing words of gold upon an ivory tablet as he goes. 'Continuing on past the Happy Groves take the well-marked track to the right, but at the third clump of asphodel, note a grassy track diverging to the left, and follow this until it leads into an open space covered with amaranth and moly.'

(Sidgwick 1912)

Boots

Boots and the Man, I sing! For you cannot tramp without boots.

The tramp gets affectionately attached to his boots when they have served him long and well ... poems addressed to boots are hard to find, and one must assume that poets for the most part do not tramp. For if they tramp there inevitably comes the pathetic moment when looking upon discarded boots by starlight the poet says: "Oh, boot, have you not served me well, old boot, old friend!" There is a lost poetry in boots - "lines addressed to my favourite boots," "lines written after taking off my most cruel boots," "lines written before putting on my boots." The last, on the occasion of putting them on swollen and blistered feet, might be the occasion of a long, reflective poem.

(Graham 1927)

"A plague on my accursed feet," thought I as I limped along the road on a broiling day feeling that every step took me nearer to the infernal regions ... my feet pained me, for my heavy boots caused blisters to spring up on my big toe. Now I know the reason why Gypsies bury a good pair of boots with a corpse. They know that the dead must wander many a weary mile over burning plains as I am doing now, and well-fitting boots are necessary. Boots are objects of veneration to wandering folk because so much depends on them. Any man who intends to set out on a long tramping tour should spend more money on his boots than on all the rest of his kit and on his journey money. I had set out from Italy with boots borrowed from a peasant and I was now suffering for my negligence, for the boots had never fitted me completely and the blisters had come. When we read fairy stories which were inspired by Gipsy wanderers we find many descriptions of magic shoes which carry men over hill and over dale. It was the Gypsies, I am sure, who invented the seven-leagued boots to give themselves courage on a tedious journey. Shoes are a symbol of fertility and the good things of this life, as any Gipsy will tell us.... Everyone knows the old nursery rhyme of the woman who lived in the shoe, but few realize its significance:

>"There was an old woman who lived in a shoe,
>
>She had so many children she did not know what to do."

(Starkie 1933)

The second great point in a walker's conversation is that his 'shop' is less shoppy and more interesting than that of other men. The minutiae of his own craft are homely and human things - boots and coats and knapsacks and hobnails and ordnance maps. The golfer's talk has only a limited interest, the motorist is little better. But all turn round with a pleased smile when a friend of mine begins the life history of his famous boots, how they were originally bought as football boots and scored twenty-seven goals in two seasons, how they were then resoled and nailed by a Swiss cobbler and went up Mont Blanc, how they subsequently covered nine hundred miles in the Home Counties, how they lost all their nails and went to a garden party, how they split on a critical occasion and were under-girded (like St. Paul's ship) with string, bootlaces, and a Government strap, how, finally, when they were past their work, they were offered to (and only refused after a struggle by) the Pitt-Rivers anthropological collection in the Oxford Museum, and how they now repose in a glass case inscribed with the words *Bene Merentibus.*

(Sidgwick 1912)

Arrived at a place about two miles from Swansea, I found that I was splashed from top to toe, for the roads were frightfully miry, and was sorry to perceive that my boots had given way at the soles, large pieces of which were sticking out. I must, however, do the poor things the justice to say, that it was no wonder that they were in this dilapidated condition, for in those boots I had walked at least two hundred miles, over all kinds of paths, since I had got them soled at Llangollen.

As soon as I was shown into the parlour I summoned the "boots", and on his making his appearance I said in a stern voice: "My boots want soling, let them be done by tomorrow morning."

"Can't be, sir, it's now Saturday afternoon, and the shoemaker couldn't begin them to-night!"

"But you must make him!" said I, "and look here, I shall give him a shilling extra, and you an extra shilling for seeing after him,"

"Yes, sir, I'll see after him - they shall be done, sir. Bring you your slippers instantly."

(Borrow 1862)

We crossed a crag-strewn valley, which was very rough on our boots. My boots were cracking, Lindsay's held out a little while longer, but mine died that day. As we each carried two pairs of boots we were prepared for the emergency.

Mine had been a stout pair of pre-war boots. I used them first in North

Norway and Russia. I tramped in them in France. They were repaired first in the Caucasus ... for the second time in Georgia. For I did Sherman's march and walked from Atlanta to the sea in them in 1919. And they were repaired for the last time by a Frenchman last year.

"We must burn them," said Vachel, "and have a special ceremony. These are no ordinary boots to be abandoned in the wilds without the meed of some melodious tear." So we burned one on a high flaming fire with young pine shoots for incense, and the other we threw into a rushing mountain torrent, and bade it continue its world journey to the world's end.

(Graham 1922)

[America 1875]

Occasionally on the sidewalk, amid the dapper, swiftly-moving, high-heeled boots and gaiters, I catch a glimpse of the naked human foot...though it be a black foot and an unwashed foot, it shall be exalted. It is a thing of life among leather, a free spirit among cramped, a wild bird among caged, an athlete among consumptives. It is the symbol of my order, the Order of Walkers.

I am going to brag as lustily as I can on behalf of the pedestrian, and show how all the shining angels second and accompany the man who goes afoot, while all the dark spirits are ever looking out for a chance to ride.

I fear, also, the American is becoming disqualified for the manly art of walking, by a falling off in the size of his foot...a small, trim foot, well booted or gaitered, is the national vanity. How we stare at the big feet of foreigners, and wonder what may be the price of leather in those countries.

(Burroughs 1875)

Heavy nailed boots used to be taken as, in every sense, the foundation of walking equipment but a formidable school of shoe-walkers has arisen, who deny the axiom of boots. The bootmen in the first exasperation of outraged orthodoxy will probably say that shoes are effeminate, while boots are the mark of a man, at which the shoemen ask, why it should be effeminate to have a soft and slight covering between the feet and reality and manly to have several layers of bull's hide clamped with armour plating. Somewhat sobered, the bootmen then say that boots support the ankles, to which the shoemen reply that their ankles do not need supporting. This innuendo finally makes the bootmen think, and they issue from their meditations with the unanswerable remark that shoes let stones in and boots do not. The shoemen, if they are wise, admit this, merely adding, that if shoes let stones in they can easily be taken off and shaken, and that if boots keep stones out, they also keep air out.

The bootmen then take the aggressive: if air is wanted, why walk at all? Why not stand on your head with your feet out of the window? To which the shoemen say, Don't be silly, and the bootmen say, You have no sense of humour, and the relations of years are dissolved.

(Sidgwick 1912)

I was determined to walk to Brindisi, so I set forth next morning. Eventually I arrived in Brindisi but only after falling a victim to sore feet. The tutelary genius of the Via Appia, alas, is unkind to pedestrians, and laid me low at Francavilla. While I was resting dejectedly by the side of the road, an old peasant passed by in a cart, and catching sight of my sore foot, which I had relieved of its sock and shoe, he said,

"Have you been wounded?"

"My feet have given out," I said piteously.

"I'll cure them for you," he said, "climb up." He took me to his cottage a little further along the road. He put me sitting under a tree in the yard and went to fetch his wife, saying "We'll get our Saint to cure you." He returned followed by a grey-haired woman carrying a bottle.

"Show me your foot," she said. "Saint Nicholas will soon cure it."

"Who is Saint Nicholas?" I asked.

"Have you never heard of Saint Nicholas of Bari? You ought to be ashamed of risking yourself on the roads without his protection. He can even raise a man from the dead, and as for sickness - there isn't a disease sent to us from Satan that Saint Nicholas won't cure."

With these words she opened the bottle and poured some oil on my foot. "This oil," she said, as she rubbed it tenderly, "is indeed a miraculous manna. I procured several bottles of it on the eighth of May last when I made a pilgrimage to the crypt of San Nicola in Bari."

Thanks to good St. Nicholas I was able to accomplish my foot-slogging trek to Brindisi, which I entered singing to myself the last verses of his hymn:

Wherefore sing hymns in praise of St. Nicholas,

for he who drives away his vices and prays to him,

will return safe and sound. Amen.

(Starkie 1933)

Personally, I can see nothing wrong with wellingtons for wet weather and plimsolls or training shoes for dry weather, that's if all you're doing is fell walking. Climbing rock faces would be another matter, but then that's mechanical engineering, nothing to do with walking. There's no mystique about walking. Walking consists of placing one foot in front of the other, taking care when coming downhill that you look where you're putting the said feet, and that's all there is to it. You don't wear climbing boots to go up and down stairs at home so why wear them for walking up a hill? If you worry that you're going to twist your ankles, either going up stairs or going up Scafell then by all means wear great huge clumping leather boots. To me, it's like taking another passenger.

(Hunter Davies 2000)

I contend that a man with a good pair of feet can walk in almost anything: boots, shoes, sandals, even carpet slippers, and go barefoot on soft ground.

(Hillaby 1972)

Many an Englishman will not understand the advantage of sandals - cloth slippers with a sole made of twisted cord ... the advantage of these is a thing of which you can never convince a man the first time he attempts these mountains [Pyrenees], but he is sure enough of it at the end of his first day. For some reason or other, the loose stones and the pointed rocks of a mule path make travel upon foot intolerably painful and difficult if it is too long pursued in ordinary boots. With sandals on, you do not feel the fatigue of a track that would finish you in 5 miles if you tried to do it in leather. And conversely, oddly enough, a high road with a good surface soon becomes as intolerable in sandals as is a mule track in boots. There is nothing for it but to leave your boots at the nearest town if you propose to return to it, or if you do not, to carry them with you and change from one foot-gear to the other as you pass from the mountain to the road and from the road to the mountain.

Remember that, in sandals, you will always end the day with wet feet. Let not that trouble you. They dry at once before the camp fire and they do not shrink.

(Belloc 1909)

My legs were soon soaking, but they didn't matter, they never do matter. My contempt for them, which amounts almost to loathing, has subjected them in their time to all manner of discomforts. Still they carry me along, faithful supporters. If they had eyes they would look at me like a couple of thrashed dogs, reproachfully.

(Wainwright 1986)

I treat my feet like premature twins.

(Hillaby 1968)

[on a long, arduous and sometimes dangerous walk]

What the attraction is, I'm not quite sure. The mystics, no doubt, would see it as a microcosm of the journey through life. A rather inflated claim. There have, however been times at the end of a rain-sodden day when heaven can appear in the shape of a dry pair of socks.

(Wilson 2002)

Socks

I must speak of socks. Those who know most about marching, wear none, and for marching along roads it is a sound rule (startling and unusual as that rule may sound) to have the skin of the human foot up against the animal skin of the boot, that boot being well soaked in oil and pliable. There is no form of foot covering within the boot that does not chafe and tear and therefore blister the skin, if one goes a long way at a time, and for many days of tramping on end. That is the general rule, and in the French service it is universally recognised in the infantry.

(Belloc 1909)

My one sartorial extravagance was a second pair of socks. In London, an expert traveller had pointed out that weight could be saved by carrying only one spare sock. Thus equipped with a total of three socks, the professional circulates them on the principle of crop rotation. Each morning, yesterday's right sock is moved to the left foot, yesterday's left sock is taken out of circulation for washing and mending, and yesterday's fallow sock, now clean and dry, is put on to the right foot. It is an ingenious system, but I anticipated two disadvantages: first, the diurnal rotation could become very muddling, and second, the system had the more serious drawback that the left foot would always be encased in a two-day-old sock. Reversing the direction of rotation would not be an option, since it would merely subject the right foot to the same low standard of comfort and hygiene. On balance, I decided that the extra calories I would burn by having to carry two spare ankle socks rather than one would be more than compensated for by the pleasure derived from starting each day with both feet cushioned in laundered cotton.

(Crane 1997)

Hat

The choice of hat is important. Do not take a cap. You need a brim. And do not take a straw hat. You cannot lie down comfortably with a straw hat on. A tweed hat is best. The brim has a double use. It shields your eyes from the sun, but also, when you lie down where flies and mosquitoes abound, you had best sleep in your hat, and use the brim to lift the mosquito net an inch from your face.

(Graham, 1927)

I also wore a hat, a brown battered felt object, somewhat like an old fedora, with a wide brim, and a curious leather band round the crown which gave it a backwoods character. This hat, Le Brun, besides performing the normal hat-like functions, had several magical virtues. One was deflecting lightning. Another was helping me to see in the dark. A third was giving me the most vivid dreams about Stevenson whenever I slept with it tipped over my nose.

But most important of all, perhaps, was Le Brun's power to make other people laugh. It is a vital point ... a stranger is not always a welcome figure ... But not with Le Brun. It is quite impossible to be menaced by someone wearing Le Brun. You can only smile at such an apparition - *un type au chapeau incroyable*!

(Holmes 1985)

I did make one mistake about the weather. I never got myself a proper hat. Since leaving Wallsend I'd been wearing a rather floppy suede cap which my wife bought me as a Christmas present several years ago. It never let in the rain, but during those days of incessant drizzle ... it began to sag lower and lower round my ears till eventually my neck was creaking under the weight. At each little town I tried to buy one of those fishermen's oilskin hats which I decided would be the best head covering, but I never found one. So I persevered with my ridiculous entirely unsuitable suede hat, convincing myself that if I was going to look a jerk below the neck at least my headgear was expensive.

With fussing about my hat, I missed a few archaeological goodies on the way.

(Hunter Davies 1993)

Those who wear waistcoats or hats may, of course, attempt to defend them on practical grounds: they may even say, with some truth, that waistcoats have convenient pockets, and hats keep the sun off ... If those who leave their heads bare when alone in the country, but put on their caps to pass through a village, are accused by the libertarians of inconsistency, they can justly claim that all mankind are inconsistent in this matter.

(Sidgwick 1912)

Stick

[Richard Hooker walking from Oxford to Exeter to see his mother c. 1572]

... with a companion of his own College, and both on foot, which was then either more in fashion, or want of money, or their humility made it so: but on foot they went, and took Salisbury on their way, purposely to see the good Bishop [his patron] ... and at the Bishop's parting with him, the Bishop gave him good counsel, and his benediction, but forgot to give him money, which when the Bishop had considered, he sent a servant in all haste to call Richard back to him: and at Richard's return, the Bishop said to him, "Richard, I sent for you back to lend you a horse, which hath carried me many a mile, and, I thank God, with much ease", and presently delivered into his hand a walking-staff, with which he professed he had travelled through many parts of Germany. And he said, "Richard, I do not give, but lend you my horse: be sure you be honest, and bring my horse back to me at your return this way to Oxford."

(Izaak Walton 1666)

Although I never carry a walking-stick, holding that arms are meant to be swung to increase momentum, I felt much in need of protection that morning ... I broke off a bone-dry piece of Arolla pine, near six foot in length and towards the base as thick as my arm.

On a fancy I called it Willibrord and with that fine staff in hand I strode down the stream with enormous confidence. The brute I intended it for never appeared. No doubt it saw me coming or heard me singing dog-battling songs from afar.

(Hillaby 1972)

I was now thoroughly foot-sore. One foot was particularly bad, and in trying to save it I used different muscles in the leg, which were quickly tired. Then, to help myself, I had leaned heavily on my stick at every step and so brought arm and shoulder to a state of discomfort, if not pain. Finally, the stick was unsuitable for its purpose and sorely afflicted the palm of the hand that grasped it. I had carried the stick for many single days of walking and liked it. For it was a tapered oak sapling cut in the Weald and virtually straight because its slightly spiral curves counteracted one another. But it had almost no handle, and so drove itself into one small portion of the palm when leaned on. It had also in the winter shown itself hard to retain in the hand when a few inches of it were in mud. Nevertheless, it was so nicely balanced and being oak so likely to last a lifetime that, for six years, I put up with its faults, and now, having been in my company for so many miles in a splendid June, it has a fresh hold upon me. Also I am not certain that any other handle, a larger and rounder knob or a stout natural crook, would have been much better in a hand not made of iron. Perhaps a really long staff grasped some way from its upper end would be right. But there is something too majestic, patriarchal even, about such a staff. A man would have to build up his life round about it if it had been deliberately adopted. And gradually he would become a celebrity. Of course, if he had an inclination towards such a staff, as the natural and accredited form among pedestrians, there would be an end of the matter, but that is not very likely in a town-bred Englishman. He must meditate upon what might have been, and be content to make five shillings out of his meditation, if he is a journalist.

(Edward Thomas 1913)

Umbrella

The road now lay nearly due west. Rain came on, but it was at my back, so I expanded my umbrella, flung it over my shoulder, and laughed. Oh, how a man laughs who has a good umbrella when he has the rain at his back, ay, and over his head too, and at all times when it rains except when the rain is in his face, when the umbrella is not of much service. Oh, what a good friend to a man is an umbrella in rain time, and likewise at many other times. What need he fear if a wild bull or a ferocious dog attacks him, provided he has a good umbrella? he unfurls the umbrella in the face of the bull or dog, and the brute turns round quite scared and runs away. Or if a footpad asks him for his money, what need he care provided he has an umbrella? he threatens to dodge the ferrule into the ruffian's eye, and the fellow starts back and says, "Lord, sir! I meant no harm. I never saw you before in all my life. I merely meant a little fun." Moreover, who doubts that you are a respectable character provided you have an umbrella? you go into a public-house and call for a pot of beer, and the publican puts it down before you with one hand without holding out the other for the money, for he sees that you have an umbrella and consequently property. And what respectable man when you overtake him on the way and speak to him will refuse to hold conversation with you, provided you have an umbrella? No one. The respectable man sees you have an umbrella and concludes that you do not intend to rob him, and with justice, for robbers never carry umbrellas. Oh, a tent, a shield, a lance, and a voucher for character is an umbrella. Amongst the very best friends of man must be reckoned an umbrella.

(Borrow 1862)

[The ascent of the Riffelberg]

The expedition consisted of 198 persons, including the mules, or 205, including the cows.

As follows:

It was full four o'clock in the afternoon before my cavalcade was entirely ready. At that hour it began to move. In point of numbers and spectacular effect it was the most imposing expedition that had ever marched from Zermatt.

I commanded the chief guide to arrange the men and animals in single file, twelve feet apart, and lash them all together on a strong rope. He objected that the first two miles was a dead level, with plenty of room, and that the rope was never used except in very dangerous places. But I would not listen to that. My reading had taught me that many serious accidents had happened in the Alps simply from not having the people tied up soon enough, I was not going to add one to the list. The guide then obeyed my order.

When the procession stood at ease, roped together, and ready to move, I never saw a finer sight. It was 3,122 feet long - over half a mile, every man but Harris [his agent] and me was on foot, and had on his green veil and his blue goggles, and his white rag around his hat, and his coil of rope over one shoulder and under the other, and his ice-axe in his belt, and carried his alpenstock in his left hand, his umbrella (closed) in his right, and his crutches slung at his back. The burdens of the pack mules and the horns of the cows were decked with the Edelweiss and the Alpine rose.

I and my agent were the only persons mounted. We were in the post of danger in the extreme rear, and tied securely to five guides apiece. Our armour-bearers carried our ice-axes, alpenstocks, and other implements for us. We were mounted upon very small donkeys, as a measure of safety, in time of peril we could straighten our legs and stand up, and let the donkey walk from under. Still, I cannot recommend this sort of animal - at least for excursions of mere pleasure - because his ears interrupt the view. I and my agent possessed the regulation mountaineering costumes, but concluded to leave them behind. Out of respect for the great number of tourists of both sexes who would be assembled in front of the hotels to see us pass, and also out of respect for the many tourists whom we expected to encounter on our expedition, we decided to make the ascent in evening dress.

At fifteen minutes past four I gave the command to move, and my subordinates passed it along the line. The great crowd in front of the Monte Rosa hotel parted in twain, with a cheer, as the procession approached, and as the head of it was filing by I gave the order, 'Unlimber - make ready - HOIST!' and with one impulse up went my half mile of umbrellas. It was a beautiful sight, and a total surprise to the spectators. Nothing like that had ever been seen in the Alps before.

(Mark Twain 1880)

Books

Never start on a walking tour without an author whom you love ... no one, indeed, wants to read much after a long walk, but for a few minutes, at supper or after it, you may be in the seventh heaven...

(Trevelyan 1913)

Unless a man always carries a book with him, when he does take one it is often a little too well chosen, or rather chosen too deliberately, because it is a very good one, or is just the right one, or is one that ought to be read. But walking is apt to relieve him of the kind of conscience that obeys such choices. At best he opens the book and yawns and shuts it. He may then look about him for any distraction rather than this book. He reads through a country newspaper, beginning and ending with the advertisements. He looks at every picture in an illustrated magazine. He looks out of the window for some temptation ... If he opens the choice book he finds in it an irresistible command to go to bed at nine o'clock. The same book may be taken out thus a score of times, and acquire a friendly and well-read appearance.

(Edward Thomas 1913)

What greater joy in the world than to roam arm-in-arm with the immortal characters of literature. When I am in the town I should never dare to knock at the back door of Don Quixote's house or at the palace gate of Pantagruel, but out here in the bare country on this endless spring day, I may buttonhole them and hold as many quips and cranks with them as I will. It is only when walking that we may justly appraise an author. If anyone tells me that so and so is a great character of fiction, I would straightway reply - "Yes, but have you travelled with him? What do you think of him when you've tramped five miles with him? What do you think of him when you've an empty belly? Or when you're drunk, sober, drenched to the skin, bug-ridden, lousy, and stiff with the cold? Only by such tests may you decide whether to kick him into the dusty, shadowy, cobweb-ridden limbo, or crown him with a garland of wild flowers and gather him into your family as guide, philosopher and friend."

(Starkie 1936)

Food and drink

The second topic of conversation, which is especially the property of walkers, is the topic of food and drink. This, like the weather, is generally taboo in polite circles ... Viewed in isolation, a meal is not much, viewed in its relation to the day and the day's work, it is an interesting, important, even essential element. What walker is there who does not treasure in his inmost heart the memory of some chocolate consumed on a mountain top, some stream drunk dry among the eternal hills, some sandwich eaten in a palpitating shadow-land of shifting mist. Such memories are indeed part of his being: and when they issue forth in conversation they come with no glutton's levity, but with the gravity of the whole nature of man.

There is one further cause which tends to set apart the walker's food and his conversation about it, from that of other men, he usually carries it, at least for the midday meal or meals, on his person. It is thus far more intimately associated with him than the food which issues at stated intervals from the mysterious economy of the home ... Better a simple marmalade sandwich which has climbed a hill with you firmly stuck to your pouch and your ordnance map, than all the flesh-pots of Egypt ...

To the gourmet food and drink are regarded merely as ticklers of the palate, and not as builders and preservers of the body. Now surely this is once more an error of abstraction. Properly regarded, the sandwich does not cease when it is swallowed, it gives shape and colour to the subsequent pipe: it braces the heart for the afternoon walk, its swan song calls us to tea, last of all, its spirit is linked and welded into the imperishable memories of the day. Can the gourmet say the same of his lobster salad? Is it not, when once its brief domination of the palate is over, at best a fruitless and dissociated memory, at worst a torment and a foe?

(Sidgwick 1912)

Another great pleasure of the road is the solitary meal and smoke, which brings a sense of placid contentment and sleepy well-being to the wanderer. When I set out, I took care to store my knapsack with a large piece of roast chicken as an extra delicacy for the journey. All the morning, as I walked, thoughts of that roast chicken kept stealing into my mind, like an ever-recurring theme of music. It was, as I said, an extra tit-bit, for a wanderer, as a rule, does not carry chicken in his knapsack. Instead, he stores it with the indispensable rations - raw ham, which corresponds to the bully-beef of war days, sprigs of garlic, which is not only a dainty, but also the universal medicine, and finally cheese, which, with bread and wine, is the staple diet of a tramp.

Let no one think that red wine tastes bitter out of a wineskin, when the traveller has rinsed it well with sugar and water ... wine tastes better out of a skin than out of a decanter, because the sun and the heat of the body warms the pigskin and quickens the flavour. But copious draughts of red wine out of warm pigskin intoxicate more easily, because the sun's rays stir the fermented juice of the grape to rebellious activity. Dionysus, in the torrid hour of noon, is the most dangerous of all the gods. When I wiped my wine-stained mouth and rose to my feet to continue my journey, I stumbled uneasily along the road. The countryside had changed in the meantime, or was it my eye that refused to focus normally? The sun was redder and fiercer and my face flushed a deeper dye in sympathy. Where was the freshness of the early morning...

(Starkie 1934)

You must have ample provision. The first element of this is bread, and you will do well to allow a pound and a half per man per day. Those are the rations of the French army and they are wise ones. If each man of a party carries a four pound loaf, you have just enough, but not too much for accidents. A man must have bread, he can do without meat, and at a pinch he can do without wine, but I know by experience that he cannot depend upon any form of concentrated food to take the place of the solid wheaten stuff of Europe. Half a pound of bread and a pint of wine is a meal that will carry one for miles, and nothing can take their place. For meat, you will carry what the French call Saucisson, and the Spaniards, Salpichon. You will soon hate it, even if you do not, as is most likely hate it from the bottom of your heart on the first day, but there is nothing else so compact and useful. It is salt pig and garlic rolled into a tight hard sausage which you may cut into thin slices with a knife, and it is wonderfully sustaining. If you like to carry other meat do so, but you can live on Salpichon and it means less weight than meat in any other form.

These two, bread and saucisson, are the essentials of provision, but other provision hardly less essential should be added to them, and the first of these extras is Maggi. Maggi is a sort of concentrated beef essence ... packed in little oblong capsules which you buy by the dozen, at about 1d. a capsule, and you would do well to start with three or four dozen a man. You can, with two capsules to a quart of water, make in a few moments a hot and comforting soup which quite doubles the nourishment of your bread, with three capsules to a quart of water you have a very strong soup, which will bring a man round a corner of extreme fatigue.

(Belloc 1909)

I opened a tin of Bologna sausage and broke a cake of chocolate, and that was all I had to eat. It may sound offensive, but I ate them together, bite by bite, by way of bread and meat. All I had to wash down this revolting mixture was neat brandy: a revolting beverage in itself. But I was rare and hungry, ate well, and smoked one of the best cigarettes in my experience.

(Stevenson 1896)

I have often noticed that my requirements of an inn vary according to the distance I have walked. Pleasure in these matters is like space and time, it is merely relative. When the day starts and I set off, nothing less would do than roast chicken and a cream flan. But when the miles have become longer, and the knapsack seems to have filled itself with stones, and the blisters have broadened, why, to slump into a hard chair and find fish and chips and a bottle of pop on the table represents the highest desiderata this side of heaven.

(Potts 1949)

How one enjoys one's supper at one's inn after a good day's walk, provided one has the proud and glorious consciousness of being able to pay one's reckoning on the morrow!

(Borrow 1862)

Lardy cakes ... those tough, sweet slabs of larded pastry ... they are mentioned with some indignity as a ploughboy's delicacy. My lips water for them ... four lardy cakes for threepence-halfpenny. Lardy cakes, I now discover for the first time, have this merit besides their excellent taste and provision of much pleasant but not finical labour for the teeth, that one is enough at a time, and that four will, therefore, take a man quite a long way upon the roads of England.

(Edward Thomas 1909)

And what did this philosopher think about?

He thought with growing enthusiasm that, in a side pocket of his rucksac, among the maps and a guide-book, an extra pair of socks, a jack-knife, magnifying glass, binoculars and some squashed sandwiches, there nestled a quarter of transparent malt, the finest in Glen Fiddich and a small silver tassie, and within a quarter of an hour the sun had begun to shine, faintly. The mist lifted and from both within and without he felt increasing warmth towards God, man and the cosmos.

(Hillaby 1976)

As for brandy, the people of the hills themselves discourage its use, it is, on the whole, best to have some with you, only you must not depend upon it, it is quite honestly, under the circumstances of climbing, what some foolish fanatics think it under all conditions, that is, a medicine. If you take it when you do not need it, it will fatigue you, especially in high places.

(Belloc 1909)

Be not shocked, temperate reader! In Italy wine is not a luxury of doubtful omen, but a necessary part of that good country's food. And if you have walked twenty-five miles and are going on again afterwards, you can imbibe Falstaffian potions and still be as lithe and ready for the field as Prince Hal at Shrewsbury. Remember also that in the Latin village tea is in default. And how could you walk the last ten miles without tea? By a providential ordering wine in Italy is like tea in England, recuperative and innocent of later reaction.

If I have praised wine in Italy, by how much more shall I praise tea in England! - the charmed cup that prolongs the pleasure of the walk and its actual distance by the last, best spell of miles. Before modern times there was Walking, but not the perfection of Walking, because there was no tea.

No, let the swart Italian crush his grape! But grant to me, ye Muses, for heart's ease, at four o'clock or five, wasp-waisted with hunger and faint with long four mile an hour, to enter the open door of a lane-side inn and ask the jolly hostess if she can give me three boiled eggs with my tea - and let her answer "yes". Then for an hour's perfect rest and recovery, while I draw from my pocket some small well-thumbed volume, discoloured by many rains and rivers, so that some familiar, immortal spirit may sit beside me at the board. There is true luxury of mind and body! Then on again into the night if it be winter, or into the dusk falling or still but threatened - joyful, a man remade.

(Trevelyan 1913)

You can walk further after tea, but coffee makes you more sociable ... tea indoors is very different from tea out of doors. As a domestic drink it is productive of high spirits, but out of doors it enkindles purpose. You walk and think and are silent ... but after coffee you cannot keep anything to yourself, and if you have no companion you take to singing.

Sun, moon, forest, river, road - these pass, but the coffee-pot remains. It is so in life generally, and the tramp, however much a poet he may be, is a mortal like the rest of us. The moon may be hidden by a cloud, but that is not nearly so calamitous as having left the coffee-pot at the last camping-place.

(Graham 1927)

You take a stone which has never seen either sunset or sunrise, a stone lying at the feet of trees not less than 100 feet high. It must have lain there not less than 4000 years and listened to the music of a waterfall. That is the important point. Any decent coffee beans ground in any kind of clean grinder will do. A pot that has seen more than one continent is preferred. You then cut a square piece of white mosquito net sufficient to hold the coffee and the stone. Tie up carefully like a plum-pudding, but leave seven or eight inches of string attached to it so that you can pull the coffee sack up and down in the pot at will ... the coffee must go right under.

It is prepared, moreover, in silence and without fear of flame and smoke. The pot stands on a funeral pyre, and is allowed to lift its lid several times before a hand swathed up in a towel darts in to rescue it.

We pour it out into our tin cups. It is black, it is good, it has a kick like a mule, it searches the vitals and chases out the damps, it comforts the spine and gives tone to the heart.

(Graham 1922)

CHAPTER 8

DID YOU WALK ALONE?

Walking alone is, of course, on a much lower moral plane than walking in company ... and the solitary walker, if he is honest, will at once resign all claim to the halo of patriotism, disinterested devotion, esprit de corps and good citizenship which encircles the brow of the footballer.

Walking alone, then, is a thing only to be justified by special circumstances, it is an abnormal function of life, a subject for pathology rather than physiology. But as life is not yet quite perfect, there is a place for pathology ... conditions under which walking alone is defensible if not laudable [for] the solitary walker, pursuing his lonely way under the ban of moral disapproval.

I will not even pray in aid the great names of Stevenson and Hazlitt. Their defence of solitary walking rested largely on the mistaken idea that if you walk in company you are bound to talk, they did not realise that even silence can be corporate, nay, that there is a concrete and positive taciturnity of two far more satisfying than the negative voicelessness of one. They did not know how grunts can reveal the man and ejaculations create and foster friendship. The silent contemplation of walking is aided, not hindered, by the presence of another silent contemplator at your side.

(Sidgwick 1912)

Now, to be properly enjoyed, a walking tour should be gone upon alone. If you go in a company, or even in pairs, it is no longer a walking tour in anything but name, it is something else and more in the nature of a picnic. A walking tour should be gone upon alone, because freedom is of the essence, because you should be able to stop and go on, and follow this way or that, as the freak takes you, and because you must have your own pace, and neither trot alongside a champion walker, nor mince in time with a girl. And then you must be open to all impressions and let your thoughts take colour from what you see. You should be as a pipe for any wind to play on. "I cannot see the wit," says Hazlitt, "of walking and talking at the same time. When I am in the country, I wish to vegetate like the country," - which is the gist of all that can be said upon the matter. There should be no cackle of voices at your elbow, to jar on the meditative silence of the morning. And so long as a man is reasoning he cannot surrender himself to that fine intoxication that comes of much motion in the open air, that begins in a sort of dazzle and sluggishness of the brain, and ends in a peace that passes comprehension.

(Stevenson 1889)

One of the pleasantest things in the world is going on a journey, but I like to go by myself.

I can enjoy society in a room, but out of doors nature is company enough for me. I am never less alone than when alone. I cannot see the wit of walking and talking at the same time. When I am in the country, I wish to vegetate like the country. I am not for criticising hedgerows and black cattle...

Give me the clear blue sky over my head and the green turf beneath my feet, a winding road before me, and a three hours march to dinner - and then to thinking! It is hard if I cannot start some game on these lone heaths. I laugh, I run, I leap, I sing for joy ... I begin to feel, think, and be myself again. Instead of an awkward silence, broken by attempts at wit or dull commonplace, mine is that undisturbed silence of the heart which alone is perfect eloquence...

Is not this wild rose sweet without a comment? Does not this daisy leap to my heart set in its coat of emerald? Yet if I were to explain to you the circumstance that has so endeared it to me, you would only smile. Had I not better, then, keep it to myself, and let it serve me to brood over, from here to yonder craggy point, and from thence onward to the far-distant horizon? I should be but bad company all that way, and therefore prefer being alone...

Now I never quarrel with myself, and take all my own conclusions for granted till I find it necessary to defend them against objections...

To give way to our feelings before company seems extravagance or affectation, and, on the other hand, to have to unravel this mystery of our being at every turn, and to make others take an equal interest in it (otherwise the end is not answered), is a task to which few are competent ...

I grant there is one subject on which it is pleasant to talk on a journey, and that it, what we shall have for supper when we get to our inn at night. The open air improves this sort of conversation or friendly altercation, by setting a keener edge on appetite. Every mile of the road heightens the flavour of the viands we expect at the end of it ... What a delicate speculation it is, after drinking whole goblets of tea, and letting the fumes ascend into the brain, to sit considering what we shall have for supper - eggs and a rasher, a rabbit smothered in onions, or an excellent veal cutlet!

It was on the 10th of April 1798, that I sat down to a volume of the *New Heloise*, at the inn at Llangollen, over a bottle of sherry and a cold chicken. The letter I chose was that in which St. Preux describes his feelings as he first caught a glimpse from the heights of the Jura of the Pays de Vaud, which I had brought with me as a *bon bouche* to crown the evening with. It was my birthday, and I had for the first time come to visit this delightful spot ... on passing a certain point you come all at once upon the valley, which opens like an amphitheatre, broad, barren hills rising in majestic state on either side, with "green upland swells that echo to the bleat of flocks" below, and the river Dee babbling over its stony bed in the midst of them. The valley at this time "glittered green with sunny showers", and a budding ash-tree dipped its tender branches in the chiding stream.

(Hazlitt 1822)

[Hazlitt]

His essay is so good that there should be a tax levied on all who have not read it ... notice how learned he is in the theory of walking tours. He is none of your athletic men in purple stockings, who walk their fifty miles a day: three hours' march is his ideal.

And then he must have a winding road, the epicure!

Yet there is one thing I object to in these words of his, one thing in the great master's practice that seems to me not wholly wise. I do not approve of that leaping and running ... they both shake up the brain out of its glorious open-air confusion, and they both break the pace. Uneven walking

is not so agreeable to the body, and it distracts and irritates the mind. Whereas, when once you have fallen into an equable stride it requires no conscious thought from you to keep it up, and yet it prevents you from thinking earnestly of anything else.
(Stevenson 1889)

There are few peaceful pleasures in the world to be compared with the solitary tramp in the early morning when the fields are fresh and the dust on the roads has not been stirred.

As soon as I had left the town, I felt as if all the cares of the world had been lifted off my shoulders ... for the first five hours of that walk I felt not a trace of weariness, and I conversed gaily with myself. Sometimes I walked as fast as I could with a keen, rhythmic step ... at other times, when I became absorbed in my own thoughts, I would lag and drag my feet until a sharp stone would trip me up and bring me down to earth again with a bump. The great joy of walking comes when it is solitary. I have never in my life met anyone whom I should care to have as a walking companion. And as for a walking party of three or four, the mere thought of it depresses me. Everybody has his own individual walking rhythm, which refuses to adapt itself to his neighbour's. The rhythm of my walking awakens a host of thoughts and fancies in me, which I should be timid to share with a companion. As soon as I am warmed up by the exercise and I stride forward, following my regular beat, my mind divides up into several personalities, who converse amicably within the pattern of the rhythm.
(Starkie 1936)

I usually hold a conversation with myself at High Cup [Nick], in which I discuss the obtuseness of people who suppose that to talk with oneself is the mark of a madman. It can be, of course ... Next time you pass this Way - or any other lonely place - have a chat with yourself. You will surprise you. You will alarm you. You will shock you. You may weep or curse or laugh, because self-communion dredges the channel between your selves.
(Peel 1972)

[the Head Guide at Dove Cottage]
I've never had anything against my own company. There's nothing wrong in talking to sheep - it's when they talk back you should worry.
(Hunter Davies 2000)

That first day alone - and now I was really alone at last - steadily declined in excitement and vigour. As I tramped through the dust towards the Wiltshire Downs a growing reluctance weighed me down. White elder-blossom and dog-roses hung in the hedges, blank as unwritten paper, and the hot empty road - there were few motor-cars then - reflected Sunday's waste and indifference. High sulky summer sucked me towards it, offering no resistance at all. Through the solitary morning and afternoon I found myself longing for some opposition or rescue, for the sound of hurrying footsteps coming after me and family voices calling me back.

None came. I was free. I was affronted by freedom. The day's silence said, Go where you will. It's all yours. You asked for it. It's up to you now. You're on your own, and nobody's going to stop you.

(Laurie Lee 1969)

Walking alone, especially in the mountains, it is impossible not to feel what John Cowper Powys calls the larger silences of the inanimate, but when I come to think of days spent in high passes of the Alps I know that at heart a portion of my consciousness was constantly preoccupied with bearings and path-finding and flickers of doubt about what lay beyond the next crest. Sustained peace, as I understand it, comes from knowing precisely where I am, and for this there is much to be said for knowing a few walks extremely well.

(Hillaby 1976)

[in a hard place in the Dolomites]

I was in good training, but without the stimulating effect of company. Great as is the charm of solitary walks on due occasion, they produce a severe strain on the moral energies. Why, it has been asked by certain assailants of utilitarian heresies, should a man do right when there is no chance of his being found out? ... Most victoriously had I refuted that sneer, or so I fancied, when living in London with a policeman round the corner. But now, in the deep solitude of the Alps, it recurred to me with great force, and I felt inclined to accept the other horn of the dilemma. Why not break the mountaineer's code of commandments? Why not sit down in the first bit of shade, to smoke my pipe and admire the beauties of nature? ... for a moment I was in danger of lapsing into the fearful heresies in things Alpine which are popular among the fat and lazy. I struggled, however, against the meshes of false reasoning which seemed to be winding themselves tangibly round my legs, and toiled slowly upwards.

(Stephen 1894)

There is no doubt that walking in the mountains can be dangerous and walking by yourself must increase the odds of something irremediable happening.

But the skill and pleasure of mountaineering is moving safely in dangerous places and there is a particular satisfaction in navigating a tricky mist-covered passage or completing an awkward descent before an October darkness falls. This sense of satisfaction is heightened if you alone have overcome the problems. And the real plus of walking by yourself is that you see so much more. First out in the morning catches a variety of worms, largish mammals calling it a night, raptors sitting on gateposts planning the day's campaign and a variety of small furry animals scurrying for cover.

All these add colour to the margins of the mountain day, less often experienced by a small party and rarely by a regimented group of the local ramblers' association.

(Wilson 2002)

[falling in with a group of singing hikers]

With that joyful crew shouting the steps to which we were to march, it was not difficult to advance. But after I had plodded on with them for several hours I felt a longing to return to my solitary wandering ... I determined to lose them, and I hit upon an excellent expedient. I said to the oldest member of the party, who looked like a college professor out on a reducing holiday, that I was very hard up and I wondered if he could possibly lend me some money. He gave me a startled look and whispered to his companions. They then very ceremoniously lifted their hats to me and stalked away. I had broken one of the cardinal rules of good-breeding among hikers by asking for a loan of money.

(Starkie 1933)

[after meeting a solitary shepherd on a Scottish drove road]

I took a last look at the shepherd, who now seemed as dim as a dot. Our encounter had heightened what we call solitude, that is, an absence of other human beings. In reality, of course, I was not alone. Overhead, the larks abounded; all around, the sheep shone like wool-wisps; underfoot, the soil teemed with bacteria. Microbes, after all, are more numerous than men; rabbits are more prolific, flowers are more peaceable, and sponges are more contented. The road meanwhile climbed steadily, but without bringing me noticeably nearer to the next summit, though I walked at four miles an hour.

(Peel 1976)

Silence is not enough, I must have solitude for the perfect walk, which is very different from the Sunday tramp. When you are really walking, the presence of a companion ... [with] the haunting fear that he may begin to talk, disturbs the harmony of body, mind and soul when they stride along no longer conscious of their separate, jarring entities, made one together in mystic union with the earth, with the hills that still beckon, with the sunset that still shows the tufted moor under foot, with old darkness and its stars that take you to their breast with rapture when the hard ringing of heels proclaims that you have struck the final road.

Yet even in such high hours a companion may be good ... there comes back to me an evening at the end of a stubborn day, when, full of miles and wine, we two were striding towards San Marino over the crest of a high limestone moor ... one of us stripped to the waist, the warm rain falling on our heads and shoulders, our minds become mere instruments to register the goodness and harmony of things, our bodies an animated part of the earth we trod.

(Trevelyan 1913)

You may want a companion on your walking tour. Most walkers are initiated into the joys of walking in the company of others, a few of them, later on, strike into the hills alone. To feel completely free, to enjoy yourself to the uttermost, you must be alone.

It is good to have a companion on occasion ...choose only one, never more, three is a crowd anywhere.

Companionship doesn't mean having someone to talk with, it means having someone at your side. The jolly companion who makes your evenings pleasant after the day's work is by no means the perfect companion for a walking tour. Oddly enough, you must seek for those qualities which seem at variance with the accepted ideas of fraternity. The lively conversationalist, the man who shines at parties and dances, is the last man to choose, leave him where he is, he would not appreciate the strange environment of lonely places.

No, it is the quiet man you want. The best friend is the man who can walk along with you mile after mile and say not a word, in fact, silence is the great test of companionship. I refer not to the stubborn silences which create enmity, but to the understanding silences of comradeship. A look or a smile is always more expressive than the spoken word.

(Wainwright 1986)

CHAPTER 9

OR WITH COMPANIONS?

Superficial observers may think that the walker is a morose and unsociable person. Nothing can be further from the truth. Only by construing sociability in the very narrow sense of compliance with current social conventions, can you justify such a position: and even so, I would ask, are walkers the only men who have ever omitted calls or trifled with dance invitations? But if sociability is taken in its true sense as indicating a friendly attitude of mind, I say there is more of it between two walkers treading the eighteenth mile without a word spoken, than between any two diners-out talking twenty-four to the dozen, as if there were a tax on unaccompanied monologue, and a graduated super-tax on silence. When put to the ultimate test of fact this becomes clear. If you have walked with a man you will lend him tobacco, half-a-crown, nay, you will lend him your map, if you have only dined with him, I doubt if you would lend him a silk hat.

(Sidgwick 1912)

"Come, let us devise new means of happiness," said my companion. "Let us wander upstream to the silent cradle of the river. For all day long I hear the river calling my name."

And we journeyed a three days' tramp into the mountains, following the silver river upward and upward to the pure fountain of its birth...

Imagine our three days journeying, the joy of the lonely one who has found a companion, the sharing of happiness that is doubling it, the beauty to live in, the little daintinesses and prettinesses of Nature to point out, the morning, sun-decked and dewy, the wide happiness of noon, the shadows of the great rocks where we rested, and the flash of the green and silver river tumbling outside in the sunshine, quiescent evening and the old age of the day, sunset, and the remembrance of the day's glory, the pathos of looking back to the golden morning.

(Graham 1912)

All the morning, as we loafed along, having a good time, other pedestrians went staving by us with vigorous strides, and with the intent and determined look of men who were walking for a wager. These wore loose knee-breeches, long yarn stockings, and hobnailed high-laced walking-shoes. They were gentlemen who would go home to England or Germany and tell how many miles they had beaten the guide-book every day. But I doubted if they ever had much real fun, outside of the mere magnificent exhilaration of the tramp through the green valleys and the breezy heights, for they were almost always alone, and even the finest scenery loses incalculably when there is no one to enjoy it with.

(Twain 1880)

A poorer walker it would have been hard to find, and on even my most prolonged wanderings the end of each day usually brought extreme fatigue. This, too, although my only companion [his wife, fifteen years older] was slow - slower than the poor proverbial snail or tortoise - and I would leave her half a mile or so behind to force my way through unkept hedges, climb hills, and explore woods and thickets to converse with every bird and shy little beast and scaly creature I could discover. But mark what follows. In the late afternoon I would be back in the road or footpath, satisfied to go slow, then slower still, until the snail in woman shape would be obliged to slacken her pace to keep me company, and even to stand still at intervals to give me needed rest.

(Hudson 1909)

The morning was as varied and bright as though it were an international or a jubilee when Raymond Price and I, flannelled and hatless, with sticks and haversacks, set out together to walk to the Worm's Head. Striding along, in step, we ... struck a letterbox with our sticks, and bullied our way through a crowd of day trippers.

'Why can't those bus lizards walk?' Ray said.

'They were born too tired,' I said.

We went on up Skerry Road at a great speed, our haversacks jumping on our backs. We rapped on every gate to give a terrific walker's benediction to the people in the choking houses ... Tossing the sounds and smells of the town from us with the swing of our shoulders and loose-limbed strides...

'There's a different air here. You breathe. It's like the country,' Ray said, 'and a bit of the sea mixed. Draw it down it'll blow off the nicotine.'

He spat in his hand. 'Still town grey,' he said.

He put back the spit in his mouth and we walked on with our heads high.

By this time we were three miles from the town ... Hot-faced and wet-browed, we grinned at each other. Already the day had brought us close as truants, we were running away, or walking with pride and mischief, arrogantly from the streets that owned us into the unpredictable country ... A bird's dropping fell on a fence. It was one in the eye for the town.

'A couple of wanderers in wild Wales,' Ray said, winking. He slapped my haversack and straightened his shoulders. 'Come on. Let's be going.' We walked uphill faster than before.

'God, I like this!' said Ray. On the first rise of the dusty road through the spreading heathered common, he shaded his eyes and looked all round him, smoking like a chimney and pointing with his Irish stick at the distant clumps of trees and sights of the sea between them.

Side by side, thrashing the low banks, we marched down the very middle of the road, and Ray saw a rabbit running. 'You wouldn't think this was near town. It's wild.'

Alone on the long road, the common in the heat mist wasting for miles on either side, we walked on under the afternoon sun, growing thirsty and drowsy but never slowing our pace.

The wild common, six miles and a bit from the town, lay back without a figure on it, and, under the trees, smoking hard to keep the gnats away, we leant against a trunk and talked like men, on the edge of an untrodden place, who have not seen another man for years.

Up the road and out of the wood, and a double-decker roared behind us.

We both held up our sticks to stop it.

'Why did you stop the bus?' Ray said, when we were sitting upstairs. 'This was a walking holiday.'

'You stopped it as well.'

We opened our haversacks and shared the sandwiches and hard-boiled eggs and meat paste and drank from the thermos in turns.

'This is the way to see the country.'

At the entrance to Rhossilli we pushed the conductor's bell and stopped the bus, and walked, with springing steps, the few hundred yards to the village.

'We've done it in pretty good time,' said Ray.

'I think it's a record,' I said.

(Dylan Thomas 1940)

It is sometimes thought that a test of friendship is the ease and frequency of conversation upon lofty and abstract themes. For myself, I set little store by the friendship of two men or women who talk largely of life and death and the beginnings of things ... but when two men talk freely about food and drink, then you may be sure that a real intimacy has begun, and when a youth and maiden talk thus, their feet are on the high road to the great adventure.

Recently I overheard Mr. Jones say to Miss Robinson, 'Hard-boiled eggs are all very well for a family party, but not much good if you mean real business', to which she answered, 'I only like them on mountains in the winter.' Finding that my friends - a deplorable and indeed indefensible practice - were offering seven to two against the engagement, I caused some astonishment by taking the odds.

(Sidgwick 1912)

I have not often enjoyed a more serene possession of myself, not felt more independent of material aids ... I thought I had rediscovered one of those truths which are revealed to savages and hid from political economists:

at the least, I had discovered a new pleasure for myself. And yet even while I was exulting in my solitude I became aware of a strange lack. I wished a companion to lie near me in the starlight, silent and not moving, but ever within touch. For there is fellowship more quiet even than solitude, and which, rightly understood, is solitude made perfect. And to live out of doors with the woman a man loves is of all lives the most complete and free.

(Stevenson 1896)

Walking Out

To many people the phrase suggests people who walk out perforce because they have nowhere else to go ... but there are hundreds and thousands, who, with ample opportunities for sitting down together indoors at night, prefer to walk together in the open by day ... they have interposed between ordinary friendship and full engagement a provisional status, allowing an intimacy but committing neither party, and the name of the status is Walking Out ... walking in the open to thrash out in the cool air the question whether or no.

The best description of Walking Out is in Browning's 'Last Ride Together'. It is true that he wrote it about riding, but I am sure that this was really a mistake. Any one who has ever started on a walk after a hard week's work can only admit one interpretation of the lines:

My soul

Smoothed itself out, a long-cramped scroll,

Freshening and fluttering in the wind.

It may have been simply a printer's error: by adding two letters we can set the matter right:

And heaven just prove that I and she

Stride, stride together, forever stride.

This at least was what the young gentleman was saying to the young lady that afternoon, when I overtook them just short of Newland's Corner. It is a grassy track, and it was well that I stepped on a stick.

(Sidgwick 1912)

After school about 12.20 I started to walk over the hills. The mountain and the great valley were blue with mist and the sun shone brilliantly upon the hill and the golden fern. I had put a flask of ginger wine in my pocket and a sandwich of bread and bacon which I ate by the bridge at the meeting of the three parishes and wished I had another for I was as hungry as a hunter ... the heather bloom was long over and the heather was dark, speckled with the little round white bells. I looked for Abiasula along the green ride narrowing between the fern and heather, and looked for her again at the Fforest, but the great heather slopes were lonely, nothing was moving, the cottage was silent and deserted, the dark beautiful face, the wild black hair and beautiful wild eyes of the mountain child were nowhere to be seen.

Round the great dark heather-covered shoulder of the mountain swept the green ride descending deeply to the Fuallt farm and fold and the valley opened still more wide and fair. The beautiful Glasnant came leaping and rushing down its lovely dingle, a flood of molten silver and crystal fringed by groups of silver birches and alders, and here and there a solitary tree rising from the bright green sward along the banks of the brook and drooping over the stream which seemed to come out of a fairy land of blue valley depths and distances and tufted woods of green and gold and crimson and russet brown.

(Kilvert 13 October 1871)

O maid with hair unbound and free

Adown your shoulders flowing,

To you from all the world and me

I feel a debt is owing:

So take this little song I sing.

Writ with no hidden motive,

But just a heartfelt offering,

Mild, virginal, and votive...

You do not choke the springs of truth

With sick exotic fancies,

But breathe the mountain air of youth

Where facts are all romances.

Far from the ball-room atmosphere,

- The dark Cave of Opinion, -

There rise clean heights and summits clear,

And there is your dominion.

Far from the vapid talk of fools,

Knee-deep in purple heather,

We snap our thumbs at Grundy's rules

And breast the rise together.

from *'Saepibus in nostris'* (Sidgwick 1918a)

CHAPTER 10

WHAT DID YOU TALK ABOUT?

The walker possesses, on the average, all the conversational qualities of ordinary men, and, in addition, has certain special advantages. Walkers generalise much better than other men, whether on morals, art, or any other of the worn topics of society. Their generalities may not be so frequent or facile: but when they occur they will be far more weighty ... When you have let a problem simmer at the back of your head for the whole of a twenty mile walk, you will find at the end that it has worked itself into your system, and your verdict on it is invincible, disdaining argument and scouting refutation. What chance have the merely logical beliefs of the ordinary diner-out against the ingrown and seasoned prejudices of the walker? The rest may reason and welcome, 'tis we pedestrians know.[1]

The first great merit, then, of a walker in ordinary society is a power of authoritative and Delphic utterance on subjects which other men approach humbly with reasoning, aggregated evidence and formal disputation ... The walker by a single bold utterance of a prejudice deeply felt at once defines

---

[1] 'The rest may reason and welcome; 'tis we musicians know.' ('Abt Vogler' Robert Browning)

the position.

(Sidgwick 1912)

Now the true charm of pedestrianism does not lie in the walking, or in the scenery, but in the talking. The walking is good to time the movement of the tongue by, and to keep the blood and the brain stirred up and active, the scenery and the woodsy smells are good to bear in upon a man an unconscious and unobtrusive charm and solace to eye and soul and sense, but the supreme pleasure comes from the talk. It is no matter whether one talks wisdom or nonsense, the case is the same, the bulk of the enjoyment lies in the wagging of the gladsome jaw and the flapping of the sympathetic ear.

And what a motley variety of subjects a couple of people will casually rake over in the course of a day's tramp! There being no constraint, a change of subject is always in order, and so a body is not likely to keep pegging at a single topic until it grows tiresome. We discussed everything we knew, during the first fifteen or twenty minutes, that morning, and then branched out into the glad, free boundless realm of the things we were not certain about.

(Mark Twain 1880)

In the medicinal use of Walking, as the Sabbath-day refection of the tired town worker, companionship is good, and the more friends who join us on the tramp the merrier. For there is not time, as there is on the longer holiday or walking tour, for body and mind to attain that point of training when the higher ecstasies of Walking are felt through the whole being, those joys that crave silence and solitude. I never get better talk than in these moving Parliaments, and good talk is itself something.

(Trevelyan 1913)

No one can seriously hold that walkers are not sociable beings, capable of intimacy, responsive to good fellowship, adjustable to the conformation of each other's personality, sensitive to the fundamental unities and unaffected by the superficial diversities of men.

The real charge against walkers is not that they are unfriendly to each other, but that they fail in their duties to other people. They go walks, especially on Sunday, when they ought to be paying calls, they smoke in chairs when they ought to be in evening dress, they are in bed and sometimes even out of bed again - when they ought to be dancing.

There are plenty of social entertainments every bit as effortless socially as a walk with two familiar friends, on the other hand, there are walks with a complete or partial stranger involving much more effort and much greater hazard than any party.

Confront A. and B., previously unknown to each other, at a party. With no common experience behind them, and no common activity between them, except sitting on chairs, they have no talk, to bring their personalities into relation with each other by means of words, both being regarded as failures if the talk stops for an instant ... but send A. and B. for a walk, and the whole situation is changed. They at once have a common interest and a common activity ... they need not talk all the time ... they will learn the value of pauses, of silence, of ejaculations, even of grunts ... three miles will tell them what twenty parties cannot, whether they are destined to be friends or no. Is not a walk then a far greater social duty than a party?

(Sidgwick 1912)

An ideal companion is ideal ... but there is perhaps no greater test of friendship than going on a long tramp ... I like tramping alone, but a companion is well worth finding. He will add to the experience, perhaps double it.

You have naturally long conversations. You comment on Nature around you, and on tramping experiences. You talk of books and pictures, of poems, of people, but above all, almost inevitably, of yourself. Tramping makes you self-revelatory. And this is an enormous boon ... it will often happen that you will express yourself to yourself, as much as to your friend.

The early morning tramp is a striving time, one of reaching out, of vigorous assertions. The afternoon may mock the morning with jesting, with ribald songs. But the evening will make amends. There is a great poetic time after the camp-fire has been lit, the coffee brewed, the sleeping place laid out. You sit by the embers as the twilight deepens and talk till the stars shine brightly upon you.

(Graham 1927)

There are many forms of utterance besides talking, strictly so called: and nearly all of these are possible and even desirable concomitants of walking. Thus, there is the simple and natural babble of the first few miles, while the body is settling down to work: the intellect, so to say, is blowing off steam preparatory to a period of quiescence. Then there is monologue of the purely spontaneous kind, which asks for no listener and desires no reply - the mere happy wagging of the tongue and jaw only remotely connected with anything that could be called a meaning. There may even be relatively continuous and intelligible statements or discussions, provided that these arise naturally out of the walk and the surrounding circumstances - for example, discussions on the weather, the way, the place for lunch, the utility of hard-boiled eggs, the peculiar pungency of wedding-cake in the open air. All of these fit in easily with the walking frame of mind.

(Sidgwick 1912)

[on the Pennine Way]

... only one of my Wayside conversations cannot be paraphrased, and that was a monologue. It occurred within sight of Black Hill, when a youth emerged from misty rain, so bent by his portable mattress, frying-pan, haversack, jack-knife, transistor, and groundsheet - so snail-like, so camelesque, so bowed by the burdens of Atlas - that I supposed him to be travelling like Traherne's corn 'from everlasting to everlasting'. As the domesticated apparition loomed alongside, he exclaimed - I have his words by heart - 'Bloody awful weather'. And before I could agree, the mist had shrouded everything except the tinkle of his tinware.

(Peel 1972)

It is a fact that not once in all my life have I gone out for a walk. I have been taken out for walks, but that is another matter. Even while I trotted prattling by my nurse's side I regretted the good old days when I had, and wasn't, a perambulator. When I grew up it seemed to me that the one advantage of living in London was that nobody ever wanted me to come out for a walk. London's very drawbacks - its endless noise and hustle, its smoky air, the squalor ambushed everywhere in it - assured this one immunity. Whenever I was with friends in the country, I knew that at any moment, unless rain was actually falling, some man might suddenly say, 'Come out for a walk!' in that sharp imperative tone which he would not dream of using in any other connexion. People seem to think there is something inherently noble and virtuous in the desire to go for a walk. Any one thus desirous feels that he has a right to impose his will on whomever he sees comfortably settled in an arm-chair, reading. It is easy to say simply 'No' to an old friend. In the case of a mere acquaintance one wants some excuse. 'I wish I could, but' - nothing ever occurs to me except 'I have some letters to write.' This formula is unsatisfactory in three ways. (1) It isn't believed. (2) It compels you to rise from your chair, go to the writing-table, and sit improvising a letter to somebody until the walkmonger (just not daring to call you liar and hypocrite) shall have lumbered out of the room. (3) It won't operate on Sunday mornings. 'There's no post out till this evening' clinches the matter, and you may as well go quietly.

Walking for walking's sake may be as highly laudable and exemplary a thing as it is held to be by those who practise it. My objection to it is that it stops the brain. Many a man has professed to me that his brain never works so well as when he is swinging along the high road or over hill and dale. This boast is not confirmed by my memory of anybody who on a Sunday morning has forced me to partake of his adventure. Experience teaches me that whatever a fellow-guest may have of power to instruct or to amuse when he is sitting on a chair, or standing on a hearth-run, quickly leaves him when he takes one out for a walk. The ideas that came so thick and fast to him in any room, where are they now? where that encyclopaedic knowledge which he bore so lightly? where the kindling fancy that played like summer lighting over any topic that was started? The man's face that was so mobile is set now, gone is the light from his fine eyes. He says that A. (our host) is a thoroughly good fellow. Fifty yards further on, he adds that A. is one of the best fellows he has ever met. We tramp another furlong or so, and he says that Mrs. A. is a charming woman. Presently he adds that she is one of the most charming women he has ever known. We pass an inn. He reads vapidly aloud to me: 'The King's Arms. Licensed to sell Ales and Spirits.' I foresee that during the rest of the walk he will read aloud any inscription that occurs. We pass a milestone. He points at it with his stick, and says 'Uxminster. 11 Miles.' We turn a sharp corner at the foot of a hill. He points at the wall, and says 'Drive Slowly.' I see far ahead, on the other side of the hedge bordering the high road, a small notice-board. He sees it too. He keeps his eye on it. And in due course, 'Trespassers,' he says, 'Will Be Prosecuted.' Poor man! - mentally a wreck.

Luncheon at the A.'s, however, salves him and floats him in full sail. Behold him once more the life and soul of the party. Surely he will never, after the bitter lesson of this morning, go out for another walk. An hour later, I see him striding forth, with a new companion. I watch him out of sight. I know what he is saying. He is saying that I am rather a dull man to go-a walk with. He will presently add that I am one of the dullest men he ever went a walk with. Then he will devote himself to reading out the inscriptions.

How comes it, this immediate deterioration in those who go walking for walking's sake?

Just what happens? I take it that not by his reasoning faculties is a man urged to this enterprise. He is urged, evidently, by something in him that transcends reason, by his soul, I presume. Yes, it must be the soul that raps out the 'Quick march!' to the body. - 'Halt! Stand at ease!' interposes the brain, and 'To what destination,' it suavely asks the soul, 'and on what errand, are you sending the body?' - 'On no errand whatsoever,' the soul makes answer, 'and to no destination at all. It is just like you to be always on the look-out for some subtle ulterior motive. The body is going out because the mere fact of its doing so is a sure indication of nobility, probity, and rugged grandeur of character.' - 'Very well, Vagula, have your own wayula! But I,' says the brain, 'flatly refuse to be mixed up in this tomfoolery. I shall go to sleep till it is over.' The brain then wraps itself up in its own convolutions, and falls into a dreamless slumber from which nothing can rouse it till the body has been safely deposited indoors again.

Even if you go to some definite place, for some definite purpose, the brain would rather you took a vehicle, but it does not make a point of this, it will serve you well enough unless you are going for a walk. It won't, while your legs are vying with each other, do any deep thinking for you, nor even any close thinking, but it will do any number of small odd jobs for you willingly - provided that your legs, also, are making themselves useful, not merely bandying you about to gratify the pride of the soul. Such as it is, this essay was composed in the course of a walk, this morning. I am not one of those extremists who must have a vehicle to every destination. I never go out of my way, as it were, to avoid exercise. I take it as it comes, and I take it in good part. That valetudinarians are always chattering about it, and indulging in it to excess, is no reason for despising it. I am inclined to think that in moderation it is rather good for one, physically. But, pending a time when no people wish me to go and see them, and I have no wish to go and see anyone, and there is nothing whatever for me to do off my own premises, I never will go out for a walk.

(Beerbohm 1918)

CHAPTER 11

AND YOU SANG?

You would be astonished if I were to tell you all the grave and learned heads who have confessed to me that, when on walking tours, they sang - and sang very ill - and had a pair of red ears when the inauspicious peasant plumped into their arms from round a corner.

(Stevenson 1889)

It is the custom of many, when they get over a ridge, to begin singing. Nor did I fail, early as was the hour, to sing in passing this the second of my Apennine summits. I sang easily with an open throat everything that I could remember in praise of joy, and I did not spare the choruses of my songs, being even at pains to imitate (when they were double) the various voices of either part.

Now, so much of the Englishman was in me that, coming round a corner of rock, and finding round this corner a peasant sitting at his ease, I was ashamed. For I did not like to be overheard singing fantastic songs. But he, used to singing as a solitary pastime, greeted me, and we walked along together, pointing out to each other the glories of the world before us and exulting in the morning.

(Belloc 1902)

Nothing proves the stuff of a tune so surely as to sing it on a walk, music which can stand this test must have some real substance in it ... a man may whistle a theme when he starts in the morning, forget all about it as he sinks into the contemplation of walking, and yet find at evening that all the day it has been working in the fabric of his thoughts, and when he hears it on an orchestra it will come to him with an added richness of meaning, with a suggestion of the wind in his ears, the shower on his face, and a large contemplation enwrapping him.

(Sidgwick 1912)

Man is a singing animal, but civilisation has silenced many songs ... yet singing is very natural, and when one takes to the road the singing impulse comes to the bosom. Lightheartedness begets song. We sing as we walk, we walk as we sing, and the kilometres fall behind. After a long spell of the forced habit of not singing one finds oneself accidentally singing, and there is surprise ... what is a tramping day if it does not liberate a voice, so that you can sing out your soul to the free sky.

(Graham 1927)

After leaving San Sebastian I began to feel a free untrammelled vagabond once more. It was a fresh, sunny morning and as I walked along the country road I conversed with myself in a loud voice. A wanderer is happiest in the morning when he sets out alone from his stuffy garret. When once he gets into the strong rhythm of tramping he is as free as the King of Nature.

As long as he stays in the town he is dependent upon others ... out here in the country I am free from all hindrances: I can talk, shout, sing, wave my stick without anybody calling me madman. The sky is blue above my head, the roads are not dusty at this early hour, the air is fresh and there are birds singing ... in the morning I am an incurable optimist, for my frugal tramp's life has banished all gloomy dyspeptic melancholy, and I am ready for any adventure that comes my way.

(Starkie 1934)

For the long distance walker few moments in life are more exhilarating than setting out after an enforced delay. It's necessary to dress up, carefully, like a bullfighter. There must be no loose straps or badly-tied boots.

Adjustments can be made when you get under way, but for the take-off the need is to swing forward with all lashed down, the muscles tingling in anticipation and the spirits high. For these heaven-sent occasions I stock a few marching tunes. I don't often sing them aloud, but from memory I can call up a complete orchestra and let the themes whirl through my head.

(Hillaby 1972)

To sing, hum, burble, whistle or generally adumbrate music is at once the distinction and the pride, the duty and the pleasure, of walkers. Under the influence of a fine day and a pleasant country the voiceless and tone-deaf have been known to emit sounds coming well within the orchestral range (interpreted liberally and so as to include the instruments of percussion), while the most moderately and modestly musical of men become on their walk encyclopaedic in their range of melody and Protean in their variety of tone-colour. There is surely some natural kinship between walking and music, the musical terms - andante, movement, accompaniment - are full of suggestive metaphor, and the sacred symbol of both arts is the wooden stick which marks the strides of the walker and pulsates to the heart-beats of the orchestra.

The most obvious ground for this kinship is rhythm. The simple beat of the foot on the ground, with the natural swing of the body above it, suggests inevitably the beat of the musical bar. It is difficult to walk for long under the sway of that regular 'one, two, one, two' without fitting a melody to it ... a good walker means an instrument in good condition, with a wide compass and a ripe quality of tone. That high A after which you strive at other times with tears and sweat comes without effort; you make trees and the mountain tops that freeze bow their heads with notes which at other times would simply make the accompanist blench; your runs sound like a bird soaring into the empyrean and not like a lame man going upstairs; your trill is at last a trill, clearly distinguishable from a yodel. And when the day is done, what singing is there like that of a walker in his bath.

(Sidgwick 1912)

What has really to be guarded against is the effect of monotony in any form, even the irritating repetition of some small unconscious personal trick. Slight resentments become magnified grotesquely during the long hours of silent effort, especially of monotonous effort, on snow, glacier, or path ... [the mountaineer] may realize its foolishness, but like the similar insistence of the refrain of some silly comic song, it becomes part of the mechanical movement in which his whole being is for the time absorbed ... song is the best outlet since it fits in with the mechanical movement while it withdraws attention from it, but song can only be employed when the ground allows of the feet moving in accord.

(Winthrop Young 1920b)

The natural beat of the foot and the bodily exhilaration of walking account for a good many of the ordinary walking songs, the cheerful melodies of simple rhythm, which recall a flagging company to courage and unison. Chief of these is the famous 'John Brown's body lies a-mouldering in his grave.' Tradition dictates that this must be sung on the principle of cumulative omission -- the first verse in full, the second without the word 'grave,' the third without 'his grave' and so on, the blanks being filled by beats of the foot. Thus in the last verse but one, the first three lines consist only of the word 'John' and seven foot-beats thrice repeated, while in the last verse of all there are twenty-three beats in complete silence, until the whole company comes in on the words, 'But his soul goes marching on.' It is a point of honour to count these beats and the pause preceding them exactly right, so as to get a unanimous attack with no false starts. For reviving the attention and good feeling of a tired company, there is nothing like John Brown, and, it may be mentioned, it will carry them over 576 paces if 'a-mouldering' is reckoned one word, or 640 if it is reckoned two, as the more orthodox hold.

(Sidgwick 1912)

Much of Elgar's music seems to me to be appropriate to the Wye and its forest and hills ... but [it is] not very helpful when a Welsh mountain has to be ascended, something infinitely more rousing is required, and when I first climbed the Black Mountains ... I threw off my tie and other city nonsense, and roared uphill to the strains of the third movement of Brahms' violin concerto, much to the consternation of the sheep, who thought they were in for another shearing.

(Potts 1949)

[on the Pennine Way]

... a transistor will sometimes become a congenial fellow-traveller, as I discovered while walking here one day, feeling very weary after several hours of rain. I sat down, while sheltering under the lee of a rock, I switched on the set, and out of it came the last movement of Bach's A minor Violin Concerto. No physical stimulus could have produced such an effect, neither rest nor food nor alcohol. I felt as Edward Thomas when he also was weary: 'And I arose, and knew that I was tired, and continued my journey.' My own journey was prodded forward by those marching violins.

(Peel 1972)

[on the Icknield Way]

The road itself was now wider than any of the neighbouring lanes. The larks were loud, the sun stood high, and I strode in rhythm with the 'Rondeau' from Mozart's rollicking Horn Concerto.

(Peel 1976)

There is one form of utterance, related to music much as babbling is related to talking, which is intimately associated with the greater moments of life - the After Lunch Song. If lunch is taken properly, that is to say lightly, without strong drink, in the open, the period which follows is the very heart of the day. The limbs are well attuned to their work, the soul has begun to receive its appropriate message: there are long hours ahead, clean food within, the face of nature without. At such a time a man can if he will, do his greatest feats of mere space-devouring. But it is better, if time permits, to abate something of the full speed, and to allow the heartfelt sensations of gratitude and content to find their natural utterance in song. It need not be an appropriate song: nay, it need not be a song at all in the ordinary sense: above all, the whole company may sing without regard to one another or to any laws of time and harmony. It is the utterance alone which matters. I remember well a party of three which climbed the northern face of the Bookham Downs on a summer Sunday, with Schubert's Müllerin cycle going in front against two distinct Sullivan operettas behind, and there was in our hearts no more thought of discord than there is between the chiff-chaff and cuckoo when the reiterated fourth of one blends with the other's major third in a different key.

(Sidgwick 1912)

Music stored away mentally and recalled under stress or in moments of ecstasy is a boon for those who walk alone.

(Hillaby 1976)

[Penhale Sands]

The arc of tawny sand extends for miles - dead flat and firm underfoot. Nobody in sight that morning. Better still, it grew brighter and stopped raining. A few gulls hung in the wind. No sound except the sea ... to crown all, the sun burst out, turning the tawny sand to crocus yellow. I sang as loud as a man can sing on his own. A dismal dawn turned into a great morning.

(Hillaby 1968)

A morning for song. The sun shone, the lake shimmered and we were packed and ready to go at half-past six ... we moved off towards the escarpment to the tune of the Soldiers' Chorus from *Faust* ... After bawling a vulgar parody ... I lapsed into an equally stentorian *Daah* (pause) *dee dee, tiddly-dee-dee-daah!* which was soon picked up by the men ... advised to sing to the camels at the beginning and the end of each day's march, I had tried 'Marching Through Georgia' with considerable success, the Chorus was even better. The rhythm fitted the rolling gait of the camels ... [they] looked as if they could have crossed the Himalayas. I sang noisily and the men added some bass and treble bits which if anything were an improvement on the original.

(Hillaby 1964)

One of the greatest aids to the amateur tramp is singing. The hard-footed, seasoned tramp does not need to sing, for his muscles are pliant and responsive, but the tiro needs to sing aloud to enable him to forget the painful creaking of his stiff joints. I had started off lustily in the morning singing in a loud voice "John Brown's Body," because it reminded me of war days and marches in France and Italy, but somehow or other "John Brown's Body" did not adapt itself to solitary tramping in peace-time. I found the rhythm flagging and unconsciously I turned to the more languid "Little Grey Home in the West." To sing that tune was a sign of weariness, for nobody can tramp in time to waltz rhythm.

(Starkie 1933)

Fellow-walkers, have nothing whatever to do with dance music! You who ply your craft by day, in the open, in easy clothes, whose thoughts roam at large over yesterday, today, tomorrow, and repose upon the sane continuity of existence, what part have you in the glamour of the waltz? You who stride from a hundred to a hundred and twenty steps to the minute, with a long swing from the hips, what have you to do with the waltz rhythm?

Between you and it there is a gulf fixed. On the further side lights shine, and patent leather slithers over the polished floor ... but on this side are hills and fields and sun and wind, and as we go we shall whistle a stave to the rhythm of our stride ... find the Allegro of the seventh symphony [Beethoven]. There is the song of walking, the sacred music of our craft. The [dotted] rhythm is the exact measure of the stride, buoyant and elastic, with the uneven note marking the hoist of the outside leg from the hip ... surely we may assign this Allegro to a day in April when we surmount some height like Wetherlam or Maiden Moor, issuing on a long ridge, and swing forward over grass and rock with the wind in our ears and the earth spread out below.

(Sidgwick 1912)

CHAPTER 12

DID YOU GET TIRED OF YOUR COMPANIONS?

Toleration for the close and prolonged company of all but a few intimates tends to diminish progressively until you can't bear the way somebody drums his fingers or repeats an irritating phrase. But at the beginning, before the hard corners of mannerisms and personality begin to stick out, all is conviviality. We go out of our way to show what companionable fellows we are...

(Hillaby 1972)

In my youth, under the spell of a literary tradition, I used to go on walking tours with a few carefully selected friends, one or two or at most three. In almost every case the walking tour killed the friendship. As day succeeded day, we grew so bored, we grew so to hate the sight of each other, that we never wanted to see one another again. On reflection I have come to the conclusion that what was the matter with these tours was simply the continual proximity. We simply could not get away from each other.

(Joad 1932)

Every one thinks he can walk, and most men never bother to discover why the excellent companion of the Sunday afternoon ramble proved a failure on a long walking tour.

The first point of manners for the man in control is that of pace. Most climbers suffer from the weakness of increasing the pace the moment they take the lead on a path, slope, or glacier. This is trying to the party, consciously or not, and wasteful. It is better that he should be thought to be getting old or lazy than that the party should be rushed inopportunely.

A second and frequent failing is the 'half step' trick. Some fifty per cent of fast walkers, whenever they walk abreast on road or path or hill, persistently keep half a stride in front, their shoulder just clear of their companion. Its effect is that the friend is perpetually straining to catch up, and the pace then steadily accelerates till both are practically racing. Then one gives up, and both lag, until the game starts again.

A third breach of manners, all too common, is passing ahead in the line of march. There are few inexperienced walkers who do not take advantage of the slightest error in the choice of route on the first man's part, to break off and pass him on the shorter line. He either runs ahead to regain his place, or he plods behind with a slight sense of injury.

On the ascent of steep slopes or open hillsides an experienced front man will probably take these on a zigzag. To a less experienced walker it is generally a temptation to cut the zigzags on the direct line, and so pass ahead. This is bad walking ... it is more politic to be considered a well-mannered tramp than to assert one's powers as a limber hill-rusher.

(Winthrop Young 1920b)

Conversation, we are often told, like letter-writing, is a lost art. We live too much in crowds. But if ever men can converse pleasantly, it is when they are invigorated by a good march: when the reserve is lowered by the long familiarity of a common pursuit, or when, if bored, you can quietly drop behind, or perhaps increase the pace sufficiently to check the breath of the persistent arguer.

(Stephen 1901)

It is possible, simultaneously to stroll and to babble, to stroll and to talk, to walk and to babble. Strolling, the mere reflex action of the legs, is compatible with that sustained and coherent activity of the mind which alone deserves the name of talking. Babbling, the corresponding reflex action of the mind, is equally compatible with that supreme activity of the whole being which men call walking. But the attempt so often made to combine real walking with real talking is disastrous. Better the man who babbles and strolls, who trails his feet across country and his tongue across commonplace, than the man who tries to ventilate fundamental things while his body is braced for the conquest of road and hill.

The utter incompatibility of walking and talking needs no further demonstration, but only (what walkers much prefer) dogmatic reiteration. Talking requires a definite activity of the mind, walking demands passivity. Talking tends to make men aware of their differences, walking rests on their identity. Talking may be the same on a fine day or on a wet day, in spring or autumn, on Snowdon or Leith Hill, walking varies according to each and every one of these conditions. Those who try to combine the two usually fail to achieve either.

Sometimes, of course, a talker may be tamed, if securely buttressed by a large company of walkers, he may be subdued by a judicious mixture of silence, irrelevance, or frivolity, or he may be carried along at such a pace that he is reduced to voicelessness, if not to a proper state of quiescent reverence. But usually a single talker in a walking company will infect the whole, he will provoke them to argument and disputation, he will expose the inmost parts of his soul and gradually allure them to a like indecency. In such a case walking goes by the board, the company either loiters and trails in clenched controversy, or, what is worse sacrilege, strides blindly across country like a herd of animals, recking little of whence they come or whither they are going, desecrating the face of nature with sophism and inference and authority and regurgitated Blue Book. At the end of such a day, what have they profited? Their gross and perishable physical frames may have been refreshed, their less gross but equally perishable minds may have been exercised: but what of their immortal being? It has been starved - between the blind swing of the legs below and the fruitless flickering of the mind above, instead of receiving, through the agency of a quiet mind and a co-ordinated body, the gentle nutriment which is its due.

(Sidgwick 1912)

You must not expect to enjoy or even notice Nature, if you make one of a chattering party; or to absorb something of Nature's spirit, if you are in the woods with the girl you love; or in deep converse along the road with a friend. Walking and talking are two good things but, for my part I agree with Hazlitt, they must not be mixed.

How in my secret soul I have hated and sometimes broken out into articulate resentment against those who think a moor the right place to air their views on Socialism or Town Planning, or who discuss Theology on the seashore ... it is a poor compliment to Nature to use her as an arena for the airing of our views; we do better to let her air our brains.

(Joad 1946)

Tourists

I studied with a philosophic eye the nature of that offensive variety of the genus of *primates*, the common tourist. His main specialties, as it seems to me from many observations, are, firstly and chiefly, a rooted aversion to mountain scenery, secondly, a total incapacity to live without *The Times*, and thirdly, a deeply seated conviction that foreigners generally are members of a secret society intended to extort money on false pretences. The cause of the travelling is wrapped in mystery.

(Stephen 1894)

We crossed a field and the fold of a farm house, scrambled down a narrow stony lane and struck the main road again. About a mile above Llanthony we descried the Abbey ruins, the dim grey pile of building in the vale below standing by the little river side among it brilliant green meadow. What was our horror on entering the enclosure to see two tourists with staves and shoulder belts all complete postured among the ruins in an attitude of admiration, one of them of course discoursing learnedly to his gaping companion and pointing out objects of interest with his stick. If there is one thing more hateful than another it is being told what to admire and having objects pointed out to one with a stick. Of all noxious animals too the most noxious is a tourist. And of all tourists the most vulgar, illbred, offensive and loathsome is the British tourist. No wonder dogs fly at them and consider them vermin to be exterminated. The most offensive part of their conduct however was that they had arrived before us and already ordered their dinner, so we had to wait till they were done.

(Kilvert 5 April 1870)

You preferred animals?

Walking brings out the true character of a man. You will not be long in finding your companion out. As his pores open his character is laid bare. His deepest and most private self will come to the top.

Hence the fastidiousness of the professional walker in choosing or admitting a companion, and hence the truth of a remark of Emerson that you will generally fare better to take your dog than to invite your neighbour. Your cur-dog is a true pedestrian, and your neighbour is very likely a small politician.

(Burroughs 1875)

Donkeys

[on the Ridge Way]

Eve and I walked out of the sacred circle at Avebury by the eastern entrance, and with the loaded Jenny started the climb up the Herepath ['path of the army'] to the Ridge Way on the crest of the downs … our main concern, at this early stage of the journey, was how Jenny was faring as a pack animal … With growing pleasure we saw her walking steadily up the hill. There even seemed a suggestion of urgency in her stride. The pace to us was quite brisk … We set off along the Ridge Way, feeling all was going splendidly … I had begun to notice vaguely that our pace seemed to be slowing, when Eve shouted, "Mind out!"

I looked round, expecting to see Jenny's long face at its usual level, but to my surprise it was nearly on the ground. She had subsided and was now slowly keeling over, with the apparent intention of rolling on her back, presumably hoping to rid herself of her load.

"Quick, get her up!" I ejaculated. "She'll break the girth!"

We heaved on her flank just as she was going, and eventually managed to get her up, where she arrived standing firmly on my foot…

We found that the suggestion of urgency had been replaced by an almost imperceptibly slowing amble. It became apparent that a hill was regarded by Jenny as a challenge, but on the level she would rather be standing still, looking contemplatively into space, than walking.

I soon found the way to overcome her tendency to slow down. If the person bringing up the rear walked slightly to the side, so as to be within view of one of Jenny's eyes, and twirled a light switch from a bush, she kept going fairly steadily, if still slowly. A touch, no more, on her hind-quarters, occasionally, completed the process.

This produced an average speed of about two and a half miles an hour. To an energetic walker this might be an infuriatingly slow pace, but I grew to like it, as it suited the spirit of the walk we were on, and I have used if for walking for pleasure ever since.

Two or three times Jenny thought of having a roll again, but we were ready for her now.

[Eve goes home after the first day, Patrick is joined by (doctor) Basil]

Jenny seemed oblivious to the weather, and appeared no more cheerful in bright sunshine than in rain. However, we noticed something that did seem to give her pleasure. If there were cows in a field, they would show the keenest interest when they espied Jenny, and would hurry across to the fence, where they would fall in alongside, and accompany us to the extent of their field ... Jenny would sometimes greet a new herd with a bray. It seemed to give our progress a grand quality to be accompanied by so many thudding hooves and tossing horns, as the cows walked purposefully along beside us. We were like a Bronze Age tribe on the move.

The three of us, the 3 D's as we called ourselves, the doctor, the dentist and the donkey, had now walked seventeen miles on this second day, and we felt that this was enough for honour.

It was lucky indeed that Jenny was generally speaking so amenable, as it would have been unthinkable to have belaboured her as Robert Louis Stevenson did Modestine. His account of the first two days of his journey in the Cevennes makes unpleasant reading for this reason, and his difficulties can be laid, to a considerable extent, at his own doorstep for having a badly designed pack, the unwieldy "sack". I think the main cause of his trouble, however, was being alone. If someone is leading confidently on the rein, it gives the donkey a certainty of intention and direction, and we found that our twirling twig technique by the other person to the side-rear gave the necessary impetus. R.L.S. obviously expected far too much from his donkey in the way of speed, as he derides his early pace of two and a half miles an hour, which was that which we, in fact, used throughout our journey.[1] After many tribulations he acquired a word of command for donkey-driving from a Frenchman. This was "Proot!" It had a stimulating effect on Modestine, being a French donkey, but, as you might expect from such an unlikely word, its effect on Jenny was nil.

---

[1] 'A man, I was told, should walk there in an hour and a half, and I thought it scarce too ambitious to suppose that a man encumbered with a donkey might cover the same distance in four hours.' (Stevenson 1896)

We were nearly at the end of our journey ... Jenny suddenly lay down and became completely motionless, with eyes closed, and with no evident sign of breathing. We were very concerned. We had become attached to Jenny on our journey. Strong and gentle - in some ways she had been the focal point of our expedition. Had we hopelessly overtaxed her?

Basil knelt down, and tried suitable places to find a donkey's pulse ... an eyelid flickered, and Jenny took a sly look to weigh up the situation. She had been doing a little play-acting. We heard later, that this is a not uncommon stratagem of donkeys. Nothing can keep as still as a donkey, with its great gift for complete inertia.

(Crampton 1969)

Mules

[in the Pyrenees]

I have heard it discussed whether a man should travel with a mule in these hills. The practice has in its favour the fact that the mountaineers, whenever they have a pack to carry and some distance to go, travel with a beast of burden. The mule goes wherever a man can go, short of sheer climbing, and it will carry provisions for some days. The expense is not heavy; a mule is saleable anywhere in these mountains, one can buy it at the beginning of a holiday and sell it at the end of one, never at a great loss, sometimes at a profit. Nevertheless, upon the whole, the mule is to be avoided. You are somewhat tied by the beast. He is not always reasonable, and feeding him, though it will be easy two days out of three, is sometimes difficult, for while he will carry many days of your provisions, he can carry but few rations of his own. With a mule one always finds one's self trying to make an inn, and that preoccupation is a great drawback to travel in the mountains. Moreover, the keep of a mule, at a Spanish inn especially, is expensive. It is a better plan to hire a mule occasionally, as one needs repose, or in order to carry any considerable weight for a short distance over some high pass.

(Belloc 1909)

All mules reared at Bonneval [in the highest inhabited valley in France] are experts at their job, for they are specially trained to deal with snow ... they are taught to drag sledges through the deepest drifts, by advancing in a series of deliberate leaps and bounds, with regular breathing intervals, and without getting flustered. Constant practice makes them extraordinarily clever at following the invisible track by sounding for it with their feet when they are perhaps wallowing up to their bellies in soft snow ... if a sledge-driver is caught in a blizzard, it is generally best for him to leave the path-finding entirely to his animals.

(Meade 1940)

Camels

My first impression was of a troupe of comedians. They lurched about as if they were drunk. One of them seemed to be partly paralysed. It tried, repeatedly, to kneel down but as soon as it leaned forward, the ridiculous back legs began to wobble and it almost fell over. Two others were trying to bolt back to wherever they had come from and were being systematically thrashed. Another blew immense frothy bubbles which burst and clung to its jowl like shaving lather. The rest were simply skittish. They pirouetted from side to side, snatched at leaves and swung their huge necks round in half-hearted attempts to bite their drivers. All of them either bellowed like cattle or made a curious high-pitched whistling noise...

In the saffron yellow of the dawn, wisps of cloud, like the tails of egrets, flared pink, caught fire and burnt out in the blinding light of the rising sun. The coats of the camels glowed. For half an hour I marched behind eight golden camels. No hunting prince went forth with greater splendour.

(Hillaby 1964)

CHAPTER 13

DID YOU EVER LOOK BACK?

[in the Lakes]

The view turning back is always a delight. Even another few steps can alter a view, change the perspective, move mountains, bring lakes out of the hat, make houses disappear, alter the shape of valleys. Certainly you're not resting. You're admiring the view.

(Hunter Davies 2000)

If I turn over the intellectual album which memory is always compiling, I find that the most distinct pictures which it contains are those of old walks ... As I look back, a long series of little vignettes presents itself, each representing a definite stage on my earthly pilgrimage summed up and embodied in a walk.

The day on which I was fully initiated into the mysteries is marked by a white stone. It was when I put on a knapsack and started from Heidelberg for a march through the Odenwald. Then I first knew the delightful sensation of independence and detachment enjoyed during a walking tour. Free from all the bothers of railway time-tables and extraneous machinery, you trust in your own legs, stop when you please, diverge into any track that takes your fancy, and drop in upon some quaint variety of human life at every inn where you put up for the night ... I kept no journal, but I could still give the narrative day by day - the sights which I dutifully admired and the very state of my bootlaces. Walking tours thus rescue a bit of one's life from oblivion.

(Stephen 1901)

The conscious experience of a tramp can be greatly increased in a pleasurable way by the use of notebooks. It is worth while keeping a record if only to remind yourself in other years. The details of your spiritual adventures fade out unless you have a good memory or an aide-memoire.

From day to day you keep your log, your day-book of the soul, and you may think at first that it is a mere record of travel and of facts, but something else will be entering into it, poetry, the new poetry of your life, and it will be evident to a seeing eye that you are gradually becoming an artist in life, you are learning the gentle art of tramping, and it is giving you an artist's joy in creation.

(Graham 1927)

Memory plays tricks as time passes, and oft times we would fain bring to mind thoughts of happier hours, but somehow they elude us. We recall, in snatches, experiences which once filled us with joy, but the fleeting years reduce them to fragments, they have no beginning and no end, and we can never forge the chain of which they are part...

It is a splendid thing to be able to shut out the world and sit quietly at home on a wintry night and spend a few hours in idle recollection, but better still to be able to reach out a hand and take from its secret drawer whenever you wish a journal which will give no less pleasure in contemplation but which in addition will marshal your thoughts in perfect order and ensure that no chapter, no verse, no sentence of your poetry is overlooked.

(Wainwright 1986)

Tom Patterson

[from the trenches (July 1915), remembering his walk from Cambridge for his last term at Marlborough (September 1913) (p.55)]

And soon, O soon, I do not doubt it,
With the body or without it,
We shall all come tumbling down
To our old wrinkled red-capped town.
Perhaps the road up Ilsley way,
The old ridge-track, will be my way.
High up among the sheep and sky,
Look down on Wantage, passing by,
And see the smoke from Swindon town,
And then full left at Liddington,
Where the four winds of heaven meet
The earth-blest traveller to greet.
And then my face is toward the south,
There is a singing on my mouth:
Away to rightward I descry
My Barbury ensconced in sky,
Far underneath the Ogbourne twins,
And at my feet the thyme and whins,
The grasses with their little crowns
Of gold, the lovely Aldbourne downs,
And that old signpost (well I knew
That crazy signpost, arms askew,
Old mother of the four grass ways).
And then my mouth is dumb with praise,
For, past the wood and chalkpit tiny,

A glimpse of Marlborough ἐρατεινή ! [lovely]

So I descend beneath the rail

To warmth and welcome and wassail.

(Sorley 12 July 1915) [he was killed three months later]

FARE WELL

When I lie where shades of darkness

Shall no more assail mine eyes,

Nor the rain make lamentation

When the wind sighs,

How will fare the world whose wonder

Was the very proof of me?

Memory fades, must the remembered

Perishing be?

Look thy last on all things lovely,

Every hour. Let no night

Seal thy sense in deathly slumber

Till to delight

Thou have paid thy utmost blessing,

Since that all things thou wouldst praise

Beauty took from those who loved them

In other days.

(Walter de la Mare 1942)

For some, maybe, the aged and infirm, the walking days are over, and to these you can only talk. But you will find, if you are fortunate, that you are not debarred from their friendship. It is not only that they may speak to you of the walks of their youth, enlarging the distances and diminishing the times, for the abasement of the present generation, while you sit admiring the kindly law of nature by which memory passes so easily into imagination. Even if they have not been walkers, there is still a kinship between you, for the sixtieth year is like the eighteenth mile - the point at which you settle into your stride for the last stage, and the essence of the preceding miles begins to distil itself into your brain, emerging clear and translucent from the turbid mass of experience.

It is in this detailed talk that the walker takes his highest flight. It may be evening, in London, in company: yet the noise of traffic dies away, the glare of the light and the babble of others drops from you: you are alone with a kindred soul and (if possible) a map spread out between you. Then point by point and detail by detail you recall and redintegrate in memory the larger moments of your life, every path that you have taken, every stone and summit on which you stood, revive and take shape under the plastic stress of your joint memories, the outline of the eternal hills stands before you, hard and high as the call of duty: once more the soft rain enwraps you or the clean wind whips you into ecstasy. For a moment, in the midst of our dividing and abstracting civilisation, you are again a man whole and concrete. This is something better than sympathetic conversation, it is the colloquy of two beings joined by a real bond: it is common talk.

The stick will stand in the corner, with mellowed memories of the miles we went together, with every dent upon it recalling the austerities of the high hills, and every tear in its bark reminding me of the rocks of the Gable and Bowfell. And in the darkest hours of urban depression I will sometimes take out that dog's-eared map and dream awhile of more spacious days, and perhaps a dried blade of grass will fall out of it to remind me that once I was a free man on the hills, and sang the Seventh Symphony to the sheep on Wetherlam.

(Sidgwick 1912)

Dream but awhile, and clouds will lift

To show the peaks at muster,

The driving shadows shape and shift

Before the hill-wind's bluster:

Below far down the earth lies spread
With all its cares and fretfulness,
But here the crumpled soul unfolds,
And every rock-strewn gully holds
The waters of Forgetfulness.
So dream, and through your dreams shall roll
The rhythm of limbs free-striding,
Which moulds your being to a whole
And heals the world's dividing,
So dream, and you shall be a man
Free on the open road again,
So dream the long night through, and wake
With better heart to rise and take
The burden of your load again.

(Sidgwick 1912)

But why use the past tense only? We are not yet old or decrepit, the earth is still firm under us, the wind yet blows, and there is a sun (we are told) still shining in the sky. Let us put on our boots and take our sticks and go forth upon the road once more. There are several new tracks which I am anxious to show you.

(Sidgwick 1912)

On a dazzling morning in the early summer of 1919 I left the bus at Buckden, in Upper Wharfedale, to carry my rucksack over the pass into Wensleydale. I was beginning a walking tour. But no ordinary one. It was my first since I had left the army, from which I had recently been demobilised, after enduring four-and-a-half years of what seemed to me its idiotic routine. I was out of uniform, a sensible civilian again, careless once more and for all as to what purple-faced grunting military men might think of me. I had an idle summer before me, after which I would go to Cambridge. But that was not all. I took with me into the dales, like an enchanted passport, a commission from the editor of the *Yorkshire Observer* to write several articles on my walking tour, to be paid for at the rate of one guinea per article. It was my first commission of the kind - though I had done some journalism before the war, as far back as my middle teens - and I have never had one since that meant half as much.

To write what I pleased about my walking tour - and to be paid for it - this was tremendous, here was a literary career. Now add up all these items of felicity - the bright morning, Upper Wharfedale, recent demobilisation, the editor's commission - imagine what you would have felt yourself, *then double it*. The track to Aysgarth - for it was still a track then - no motor road - wound up toward the blue, larks sang above the moorland grass, the little streams glittered and gurgled among the rocks, the sun was high, and a wind blew from Paradise. I walked in delight, and now after thirty years I have only to be quiet to remember, to feel that spring in my heels and my head towering in the golden air. Youth is perhaps an overpraised season, but when all things conspire for it, as they did for me then, it lives fabulously for an hour or two, rocketing into regions afterwards closed to us for ever this side of Heaven. But the articles I wrote were not up to much.

(Priestley 1951a)

APPENDIX
ARTHUR HUGH SIDGWICK (1882-1917)

Always known in the family as Hugh, Arthur Hugh Sidgwick was born on 2nd October 1882. On 17th September 1917 he died of wounds in France.

Hugh was the fourth of the five children (second son) of Arthur Sidgwick, Reader in Greek at Oxford. His uncle, Arthur's elder brother Henry, Professor of Moral Philosophy at Cambridge, was one of the founders of Newnham College, and active for many years in the Society for Psychical Research which he had founded in 1882. He was succeeded by his pupil, W.R. Sorley.[1]

Hugh's elder brother, Frank was an authority on early English lyrics and ballads. In 1908 he founded Sidgwick and Jackson Ltd., publishing anthologies of poetry, including some of his own.

Hugh was educated at the Dragon School, Oxford (1891-5), where he became Head of the School with the Headmaster's Gold Medal. He showed early signs of great literary power, and many of his poems and articles, while at school and later, were published in the school magazine, the *Draconian*. His accounts of his walk round London in 1915, before joining the army,

---

[1] Father of Charles Hamilton Sorley (pp.14, 55, 201)

were published posthumously there (Sidgwick 1918b).

In 1895 he went with the top scholarship to Winchester where he won prizes for English Verse, Greek and Latin Verse, and Mathematics. In 1901 he went up to Balliol College, Oxford, with a Classical Scholarship, and gained first-class degrees in Classics and Mathematics and the Chancellor's Prize for an English Essay:

In 1906 he was appointed a Junior Examiner under the Board of Education. On his record there he was chosen to be Private Secretary to the Permanent Secretary of the Board in 1912. This gave him access to the major educational developments that were under discussion, and he played an important part in sorting out many of the problems. If he had survived, he was assured of a high position in his chosen field - the advancement of education.

He had been active in sports at school and university - football, athletics, rowing - but his chief delight was walking. Weekend walking became particularly important during his time at the Board, where work during the week was often long and hard. This meant that he was restricted to short expeditions, and here Surrey was his favourite county. It was even possible to attain 'the proper mood of walking' by walking alone in London (p. 41).

His recollections and impressions of these walks and other related topics were published as *Walking Essays* in 1912. His love and deep knowledge of music were shown in *The Promenade Ticket* (1914), and, of his many poems, the longest, *Jones's Wedding*, was published posthumously with some of his other poems in 1918.

In 1914 he felt that the right decision for him was to join the Army, but he could not get his release from the Board until the end of 1915. To get himself fit for military service he undertook a series of walks round London at a distance of twenty miles from the city in eight days between 16 April and 11 July. The route was one of 166 miles - an average of just under twenty-one miles a day. He could carry out this walk by following for the most part country paths, but this route is lost today.

(Murray 1939)

In 1916 he joined the Army, serving in France, becoming Captain and Adjutant in the Royal Garrison Artillery. He was specially released for three months early in 1917 to help with 'particularly delicate work' on Fisher's Education Bill. While on leave he met a young woman to whom he would have proposed marriage, but no decision was made before he returned to his Battery. He was fatally wounded on 16th September 1917, and died the next day.

His last poem, on a much-folded and grubby sheet of army paper, was returned with other papers from France:

"Whither away, my comrades, walking
Round the turn in the road?
Here is jesting, strolling, talking
Lights and laughter and fun.
And yet you leave us, one by one,
Mark the line with the left foot leading,
Shoulder your packs & pass unheeding
Round the turn in the road."

"Round the turn where the stragglers cluster
Comes a rise in the road,
Up to the heights where storm-winds bluster
Joyous & keen and free,
There is no laughter or revelry
But hills to be won with a heart abiding
That beats to the rhythm of stalwart striding
Up the rise in the road."

"What at last is the prize to be won there,
At the end of the road?"
"Only this: there is wind & sun there
Rest and storm and rain,
And there is the prize for a man to gain,
A way well won in the teeth of the weather,
A way that we may tread together
To the end of the road."

Somewhere on the Elysian plain Sidgwick must walk now with his hero, Walker Miles (p. 144), as he once imagined him walking, conducted past the Happy Groves and taking, at the third clump of asphodel, the grassy track to the left until it leads out into the fields of amaranth and moly where hero and prophet and poet may tramp in fellowship together.

(Murray 1939)

BIBLIOGRAPHY

Bartlett, Judith, personal communication (1990)

Beerbohm, Max, 'Going out for a walk' (1918) in *And Even Now* (William Heinemann Ltd. 1920)

Belloc, Hilaire, *The Path to Rome* (George Allen 1902)

--- *Hills and the Sea* (Methuen 1906)

--- 'On a Hermit whom I knew' in *On Nothing and Kindred Subjects* (Methuen 1908)

--- *The Pyrenees* (Methuen 1909)

--- *The Footpath Way, an Anthology for Walkers* (Sidgwick and Jackson Ltd. 1911)

--- 'On Rest' in *This and That and the Other* (Methuen 1912a)

--- 'The Place Apart' (ibid. Methuen 1912b)

--- 'The Valley' (ibid, Methuen 1912c)

--- *The Stane Street* (Constable 1913)

--- *The Road* (T. Fisher Unwin Ltd. 1924)

Borrow, George, *Lavengro* (1851) (John Murray 1900)

--- *Wild Wales* (1862) (Collins n.d.)

Borthwick, Alastair, *Always a Little Further* (1939) (Diadem Books 1993)

Bryson, Bill, *A Walk in the Woods* (Doubleday 1997)

Buchan, John, *Memory Hold-the-Door* (Hodder and Stoughton 1940)

Burroughs, John, 'The Exhilarations of the Road' (1875) in Belloc (1911)

Collins, Wilkie, (1851) in Macdonald (1942)

Conway, W. M. *Autobiography of a Mountain Climber* (Jonathan Cape 1933)

Cox, R. Hippisley, *The Green Roads of England* (Methuen and Co. Ltd. 1914)

Crampton, Patrick, *The Prehistoric Ridge Way* (The Abbey Press 1969)

Crane, Nicholas, *Clear Waters Rising* (Viking 1996, Penguin 1997)

Davies, Hunter, *A Walk along the Tracks* (Weidenfeld and Nicolson 1982)

--- *A Walk along the Wall* (Weidenfeld and Nicolson 1993)

--- *Wainwright. The Biography* (Michael Joseph Ltd. 1995)

--- *A Walk around the Lakes* (Orion Books Ltd. 2000)

--- *The Best of Wainwright* (Frances Lincoln 2004)

Davies, W.H. *The Autobiography of a Super-Tramp* (1908) (Jonathan Cape 1952)

--- *A Poet's Pilgrimage* (Andrew Melrose Ltd. 1918)

De Quincey, Thomas, (1821) *The Confessions of an English Opium-Eater* (J. M. Dent & Sons Ltd 1907)

--- (1834) *Recollections of the Lake Poets* in Macdonald (1942)

Farjeon, Eleanor, *Magic Casements* (George Allen & Unwin Ltd. 1941)

Graham, Stephen, *A Tramp's Sketches* (Thomas Nelson and Sons Ltd. 1912)

--- *Tramping with a Poet in the Rockies* (Macmillan and Co., Ltd. 1922)

--- *The Gentle Art of Tramping* (Robert Holden and Co. Ltd., 1927)

Graves, Robert, *Fairies and Fusiliers* (A. A. Knopf 1918)

Hazlitt, William (1822) 'On going a journey' in Belloc (1911)

Hillaby, John, *Journey to the Jade Sea* (Constable & Company Ltd. 1964)

--- *Journey through Britain* (Constable & Company Ltd. 1968)

--- *Journey through Europe* (Constable & Company Ltd. 1972)

--- *Journey through Love* (Constable & Company Ltd. 1976)

Hogg, Gary, 'A 200-mile walk on the Ridge Way', *Country Life*, November 8, 1946

Holmes, Richard, *Footsteps. Adventures of a romantic Biographer* (Hodder and Stoughton Ltd., 1985)

Hudson, W. H. 'Hill Aspirations' in Lucas (1899)

--- *Afoot in England* (J. M. Dent & Sons, Ltd. 1909)

Hughes, Ted, *Lupercal* (Faber and Faber 1960)

Jefferies, Richard, *The Open Air* (Chatto and Windus 1909)

--- *The Story of my Heart* (1883) (Macmillan 1968)

Joad, C. E. M. *The Book of Joad. Under the Fifth Rib* (Faber and Faber 1932)

--- *The Untutored Townsman's Invasion of the Country* (Faber and Faber 1946)

Kenny, Anthony, *Mountains. An anthology* (John Murray 1991)

Kierkegarrd, S. (1847*) Letters* in Minshull (2000)

Kilvert, Francis, 1875 *Diary* in Macdonald (1942)

--- *Diary* (1870-79) ed. W. Plomer 3 vols (Jonathan Cape 1938, 1939, 1940)

Leach, Christopher, *Free Alone and Going* (Scholastic 1977)

Lee, Laurie, *As I Walked Out One Midsummer Morning* (André Deutsch 1969)

Lodge, David, *Therapy* (Secker and Warburg 1995)

Lucas, E. V. *The Open Road*, (1899) (Methuen and Co. 1907)

McCloy, Andrew, *Land's End to John O'Groats* (Hodder and Stoughton 1994)

Macdonald, Hugh, *On Foot, an Anthology* (OUP 1942)

Mare, Walter de la, *Collected Poems* (Faber 1942)

Marples, Morris, *Shanks's Pony, a Study of Walking* (J.M.Dent and Sons 1959)

Meade, Charles F. *Approach to the Hills* (John Murray 1940)

--- *High Mountains* (The Harvill Press 1954)

Meredith, George, *The Egoist* (1879) in Macdonald (1942)

Minshull, Duncan, *The Vintage Book of Walking, an Anthology* (Vintage 2000)

Montague, C. E. *A Hind Let Loose* (Methuen & Co. 1910)

--- *The Morning's War* (Methuen & Co. Ltd. 1913)

--- *The Right Place* (Chatto and Windus 1924)

--- in C. E. *Montague, A Memoir*, by Oliver Elton (letter 23 July 1912) Chatto & Windus 1929)

Morley, Christopher, 'The Art of Walking' in Shandygaff (1918)

Murray, Geoffrey, *The Gentle Art of Walking* (Blackie and Son 1939)

Noyce, Wilfrid, *Scholar Mountaineers. Pioneers of Parnassus* (Dennis Dobson Ltd. 1950)

Patterson, Tom, *British Medical Journal* 29 January 1977

Peel, J.H.B. *Along the Pennine Way* (Cassell and Company Ltd. 1972)

--- *Along the Green Roads of Britain* (Cassell and Company Ltd. 1976)

--- *Off the Beaten Track* (Robert Hale Ltd. 1984)

Potts, W. H. *Roaming down the Wye* (Hodder and Stoughton 1949)

Priestley, J. B. *Postscripts* (Heinemann 1940)

--- *Delight* (Heinemann 1951)

a. 'A Walking Tour'

b. 'Walk in a Pine Wood'

Rousseau, J. J. *The Confessions* (1782) (Penguin 1953)

Scott, Walter (1857) *Guy Mannering* in Belloc (1911)

Sidgwick, Arthur Hugh, *Walking Essays* (Edward Arnold 1912)

--- *Jones's Wedding and other poems* (Edward Arnold 1918a)

--- 'A Walk round London', *The Draconian*, April/August (1918b)

Solnit, Rebecca, *Wanderlust* (Verso 2001)

Sorley, Charles, 'Rain' *The Marlburian* 31 October 1912

--- Letter to his parents 21 September 1913 in The Letters of Charles Sorley (CUP 1919)

--- 'To J. B.' The Marlburian 12 July 1915

--- *Marlborough and other Poems* (Cambridge University Press 1916)

Starkie, Walter, *Raggle-Taggle* (John Murray 1933)

--- *Spanish Raggle-Taggle* (John Murray 1934)

--- *Don Gypsy* (John Murray 1936)

--- *The Road to Santiago* (John Murray 1957)

--- *Scholars and Gypsies. An Autobiography* (John Murray 1963)

Stephen, Leslie, *The Playground of Europe* (1894) (Blackwell 1936)

--- 'In Praise of Walking' (1901) in Belloc (1911)

Stevenson, Robert Louis, 'Walking Tours' in *Virginibus Puerisque* (Chatto and Windus 1889)

--- *Travels with a Donkey in the Cevennes* (1896) (William Heinemann, Ltd. 1924)

Thomas, Dylan, from 'Who do you wish was with us?' in *Portrait of the Artist as a Young Dog* (J.M.Dent and Sons 1940)

Thomas, Edward, *The South Country* (1909) (J.M.Dent and Sons 1932)

--- *The Icknield Way* (Constable & Company Ltd. 1913)

--- *Collected Poems* (Ingpen & Grant 1922)

Thomas, Helen, *World Without End* (William Heinemann Ltd. 1931)

Thoreau, H.D. 'Walking, and the Wild' (1862) in Belloc (1911)

Trevelyan, George Macaulay, *Clio, a Muse and other Essays* (1913) (Longmans, Green and Co. 1949)

--- *An Autobiography and other Essays* (Longmans, Green and Co. 1949)

Twain, Mark, *A Tramp Abroad* (1880) (Chatto & Windus n.d.)

Wainwright, A. *The Southern Fells* (Westmorland Gazette 1958)

--- *The Northern Fells* (Westmorland Gazette 1961)

--- *Fellwanderer. The Story behind the Guidebooks* (Westmorland Gazette 1966)

--- *Pennine Way Companion* (Westmorland Gazette 1968)

--- *A Coast to Coast Walk* (Westmorland Gazette 1973)

--- *A Pennine Journey* (Westmorland Gazette 1986)

Walton, Izaak, *The Life of Richard Hooker* (1666) in Belloc (1911)

Wilson, Graham, *Macc and the Art of Long Distance Walking* (Millrace 1998)

--- *Climbing Down* (Millrace 2002)

Wordsworth, W. 'Lines composed a few miles above Tintern Abbey' (July 13, 1798)

--- *The Prelude, Book Thirteenth* (1799)

--- *A Guide through the District of the Lakes in the North of England* (Hudson and Nicholson 1835)

Young, Geoffrey Winthrop, 'Introduction' to Stephen (1894) (Blackwells 1936)

--- *Mountain Craft* (Methuen 1920a)

--- 'Walking Manners' in *Mountain Craft* (1920b)

INDEX

Bartlett, Judith, 47

Beerbohn, Max, 182

Belloc, Hilaire, 16, 20, 23, 27, 28, 44, 47, 48, 50, 53, 70, 71, 76, 88, 90, 94, 98, 101, 110, 112, 114, 115, 119, 121, 123, 129, 133, 142, 143, 150, 158, 160, 183, 196

Borrow, George, 56, 69, 81, 98, 112, 113, 120, 140, 146, 154, 159

Borthwick, Alastair, 38, 110, 126, 129, 132

Bowen, Edward, 102

Bryson, Bill, 92

Buchan, John, 4

Burroughs, John, 97, 147, 194

Coleridge, Samuel Taylor, 110, 139

Collins, Wilkie, 67

Conway, W. M. 93

Cooper, Canon A.N. 106

Cox, R. Hippisley, 53

Crampton, Patrick, 196

Crane, Nicholas, 26, 28, 29, 46, 69, 101, 103, 122, 124, 129, 132, 136, 139, 151

Davies, Hunter, 58, 66, 100, 104, 111, 113, 122, 135, 138, 139, 149, 152, 165, 198

Davies, W.H. 17, 79, 133

De Quincey, Thomas, 106, 107, 121, 134

Emerson, R.W. 194

Farjeon, Eleanor, 52

Graham, Stephen, 9, 17, 20, 23, 25, 28, 42, 45, 100, 109, 115, 125, 127, 129, 130, 131, 141, 142, 145, 147, 151, 161, 171, 179, 184, 199

Graves, Robert, 16

Hazlitt, William, 164

Hillaby, John, 16, 24, 25, 27, 45, 47, 65, 70, 88, 97, 115, 133, 134, 138, 149, 150, 153, 159, 166, 185, 187, 188, 190, 197

Hogg, Gary, 53

Holmes, Richard, 136, 151

Hudson, W. H. 49, 57, 67, 77, 105, 171

Hughes, Ted, 62

Hutton, William, 105

Jefferies, Richard, 31, 34, 51, 100

Joad, C. E. M. 7, 32, 45, 49, 61, 68, 73, 102, 103, 109, 116, 125, 130, 190, 193

Kenny, Anthony, 110

Kierkegaard, S. 34

Kilvert, Francis, 10, 24, 27, 43, 58, 67, 79, 83, 175, 193

Leach, Christopher, 4

Lee, Laurie, 98, 134, 141, 166

Lodge, David, 29

Mare, Walter de la, 201

Marples, Morris, 2, 61, 139, 140

Macdonald, Hugh, 210

Meade, Charles F. 75, 92, 197

Meredith, George, 19

Montague, C. E. 7, 48, 59, 62, 63, 64, 69, 86, 87, 89, 99, 124, 130

Morley, Christopher, 19 42

Murray, Geoffrey, 35, 45, 106, 206, 208

Noyce, Wilfrid, 74

Observer (1974) 130

Patterson, Tom, 55, 65, 85, 92, 94, 126, 131, 132, 135, 139

Peel, J.H.B. 47, 49, 56, 64, 65, 80, 126, 164, 168, 180, 187

Potts, W. H. 142, 159, 186

Priestley, J.B. 48, 119, 204

Rousseau, J.-J. 36

Scott, Walter, 140

Sidgwick, Arthur Hugh, 1, 6, 8, 22, 23, 24, 33, 35, 36, 39, 40, 41, 43, 46, 49, 84, 85, 86, 95, 96, 98, 101, 102, 104, 105, 110, 111, 116, 117, 137, 144, 146, 148, 152, 157, 162, 170, 173, 175, 176, 178, 179, 180, 184, 185, 186, 187, 189, 192, 202, 203

Solnit, Rebecca, 72

Sorley, Charles, 14, 55, 201

Starkie, Walter, 2, 25, 30, 44, 77, 97, 125, 126, 131, 149, 156, 164, 167, 184, 188

Stephen, Leslie, 1, 35, 37, 40, 44, 66, 68, 74, 83, 87, 114, 117, 125, 127, 158, 166, 190, 193, 199

Stevenson, Robert Louis, 26, 108, 128, 132, 136, 138, 158, 163, 165, 174, 183, 195

Thomas, Dylan, 173

Thomas, Edward, 7, 14, 15, 18, 19, 23, 26, 31, 32, 46, 54, 99, 117, 120, 127, 143, 154, 156, 159, 187

Thomas, Helen, 32

Thoreau, H.D. 31, 45, 119

Trevelyan, G. M. 6, 11, 18, 33, 34, 58, 62, 68, 73, 76, 90, 94, 102, 103, 105, 107, 109, 113, 118, 120, 124, 128, 155, 160, 168, 178

Twain, Mark, 89, 155, 171, 178

Wainwright, A. 9, 10, 17, 21, 8, 59, 60, 64, 64, 72, 75, 78, 83, 86, 95, 96, 108, 111, 112, 114, 134, 138, 139, 142, 144, 150, 169, 199

Walton, Izaak, 152

Weeton, Ellen, 139

Wilson, Graham, 54, 108, 113, 117, 150, 167

Wordsworth, W. 11, 78, 84, 99, 107, 121, 167

Young, Geoffrey Winthrop, 112, 186, 190

Made in the USA
San Bernardino, CA
22 November 2013